The British System of Government

Books are to be returned on or before
the last date below.

LIBREX —

Researched and written by Publishing Services, Central Office of Information.

© Crown copyright material reproduced under licence from the Controller of HMSO and the Central Office of Information 1996 Applications for reproduction should be made to Crown Copyright Unit, St Clements House, 2-16 Colegate, Norwich NR3 1BQ
First published 1992
Second edition 1994

ISBN 0 11 702042 7

The Stationery
Office

Published by The Stationery Office and available from:

The Publications Centre
(mail, telephone and fax orders only)
PO Box 276, London SW8 5DT
General enquiries 0171 873 0011
Telephone orders 0171 873 9090
Fax orders 0171 873 8200

The Stationery Office Bookshops
49 High Holborn, London WC1V 6HB
(counter service and fax orders only) Fax 0171 831 1326
68-69 Bull Street, Birmingham B4 6AD 0121 236 9696 Fax 0121 236 9699
33 Wine Street, Bristol BS1 2BQ 01179 264306 Fax 01179 294515
9-21 Princess Street, Manchester M60 8AS 0161 834 7201 Fax 0161 833 0634
16 Arthur Street, Belfast BT1 4GD 0123 223 8451 Fax 0123 223 5401
The Stationery Office Oriel Bookshop,
The Friary, Cardiff CF1 4AA 01222 395548 Fax 01222 384347
71 Lothian Road, Edinburgh EH3 9AZ (counter service only)

In addition customers in Scotland may mail, telephone or fax their orders to:
Scottish Publication Sales,
South Gyle Crescent, Edinburgh EH12 9EB 0131 479 3141 Fax 0131 479 3142

Accredited Agents (see Yellow Pages)

and through good booksellers

Contents

Acknowledgments

This book has been compiled with the help of a number of organisations, including other government departments. The Central Office of Information would like to thank in particular the Cabinet Office (Office of Public Service), the Home Office, the Department of the Environment, the Northern Ireland Office and the Privy Council Office for their help in compiling this book.

Cover Photograph Credit
COI Pictures.

Introduction

This book describes the British system of government against the background of its historical development over the centuries. The role of the Monarchy, Parliament, government departments and agencies, local government and the judiciary are all outlined. The book also gives brief descriptions of the systems of government in Wales, Scotland, and Northern Ireland.

Britain's[1] relations with the European Union are also covered as are the systems of government in the Channel Islands and the Isle of Man.

[1]The term 'Britain' is used informally in this book to mean the United Kingdom of Great Britain and Northern Ireland. 'Great Britain' comprises England, Wales and Scotland.

The Development of the British System of Government

The growth of political institutions in England can be traced back to the period of Saxon rule, which lasted from the fifth century AD until the Norman Conquest in 1066. This period saw the origins of the institution of kingship, and of the idea that the king should seek the advice of a council of prominent men. The Saxons also established a network of local government areas, including shires (counties) and burghs (boroughs), which continue to influence the structure of local government.

The period of Norman rule after 1066 saw a considerable strengthening of royal control. However, the Monarchy eventually experienced difficulties in controlling the growing machinery of government. The actions of King John (1199–1216) led to opposition from the nobility and leading figures in the Church. In 1215 the barons forced the King to agree to a series of concessions embodied in a charter which became known as Magna Carta. The charter, which provided for the protection of the rights of freemen against the abuse of royal power, came to be regarded as the key expression of the rights of the community against the Crown.

The first known occurrence of the term 'Parliament' to describe the meetings of nobles to advise the king is in 1236; by the late 13th century representatives of counties and towns were also occasionally being summoned at the same time, usually to express political support, but increasingly to give consent to taxation. By the end of the 15th century Parliament existed in a form virtually recognisable today: as a body whose function was to agree to taxes and to legislate, and which consisted of two separate chambers—the House of Commons and the House of Lords.

Because Parliament by now had considerable influence over the government of the country, it was always likely to provoke political conflict with the Crown. One such clash led to the outbreak of the Civil War in 1642 between Royalist supporters and Parliament. Following the defeat of the Royalist armies and the execution of Charles I in 1649, the Monarchy and the House of Lords were abolished and the country was proclaimed a republic. However, the republican experiment came to an end in 1660, two years after the death of the 'Lord Protector', Oliver Cromwell. Charles I's son was restored to the throne as Charles II.

Charles II's successor, James II and VII (James VII of Scotland: 1685–88), sought to set aside, or at least suspend, laws that Parliament had passed. As a result, in 1688 a group of leading men invited William of Orange (a grandson of Charles I and husband of Mary, James II and VII's eldest daughter) to 'secure the infringed liberties' of the country. James fled into exile. Following the success of the revolution of 1688, Parliament in 1689 passed the Bill of Rights, which defined the rights and privileges of Parliament.

Increasingly, thereafter, parliamentary control of national finance made it impracticable for the Sovereign to ignore the wishes of Parliament. Ministers were appointed by the Sovereign, but they had to have sufficient support in the House of Commons to enable them to persuade Parliament to pass legislation and vote for taxation. The development of parties during the 18th and 19th centuries provided them with machinery for securing that support, while the personal involvement of the Monarch in policy and the day-to-day business of administration declined, leaving government in the hands of the Cabinet, presided over by a 'Prime' Minister. Since the mid-nineteenth century the Prime Minister has normally been the leader of the party with a majority in the House of Commons.

The Reform Act of 1832 altered the medieval system of parliamentary representation and standardised the qualifications for the right to vote. Subsequent reforms gave the vote to virtually all adults—women were finally enfranchised in 1918, but not on the same terms as men until 1928. The voting age for men and women was reduced from 21 to 18 in 1969.

The British Constitution

The British constitution is, to a large extent, a product of the historical events described above, and has thus evolved over many centuries. Unlike the constitutions of most other countries, it is not set out in any single document. Instead it is made up of statute law, common law (see p. 102) and conventions. (Conventions are rules and practices which are not legally enforceable but which are regarded as indispensable to the working of government; many are derived from the historical events described above.) The constitution can be altered by Act of Parliament, or by general agreement, and is thus adaptable to changing political conditions.

The organs of government overlap but can be clearly distinguished. Parliament is the legislature and the supreme authority.

The executive consists of:

—the Government: the Cabinet and other ministers responsible for national policies;

—government departments and agencies, responsible for national administration;

—local authorities, responsible for many local services; and

—public corporations, responsible for operating particular nationalised industries or other bodies, subject to ministerial control.

The judiciary determines common law and interprets statutes.

The Monarchy

The Monarchy is the oldest institution of government, going back to at least the ninth century—four centuries before Parliament and three centuries before the law courts.[2] Queen Elizabeth II is herself directly descended from King Egbert, who united England under his rule in 829. The only interruption in the history of the Monarchy was the republic, which lasted from 1649 to 1660 (see p. 3).

Today the Queen is not only head of state, but also an important symbol of national unity. The Queen's title in Britain is: 'Elizabeth the Second, by the Grace of God of the United Kingdom of Great Britain and Northern Ireland and of Her other Realms and Territories Queen, Head of the Commonwealth, Defender of the Faith'. In the Channel Islands (see p. 132) and the Isle of Man (see p. 135) the Queen is represented by a Lieutenant Governor.

The Commonwealth

Although the seat of the Monarchy is in Britain, the Queen is also head of state of a number of Commonwealth states. These include Australia, Barbados, Canada, Jamaica, New Zealand and Papua New Guinea. In each such state the Queen is represented by a Governor-General, appointed by her on the advice of the ministers of the country concerned and completely independent of the British Government. In each case the form of the royal

[2]For further details see *The Monarchy* (Aspects of Britain: HMSO, 1996).

title varies. Other Commonwealth states are republics or have their own monarchies.

In British dependent territories the Queen is usually represented by governors who are responsible to the British Government for the administration of the country concerned.

Succession

The title to the Crown is derived partly from statute and partly from common law rules of descent. Despite interruptions in the direct line of succession, the hereditary principle upon which it was founded has always been preserved.

Sons of the Sovereign have precedence over daughters in succeeding to the throne. When a daughter succeeds, she becomes Queen Regnant, and has the same powers as a king. The consort of a king takes her husband's rank and style, becoming Queen. The constitution does not give any special rank or privileges to the husband of a Queen Regnant, although in practice he fills an important role in the life of the nation, as does the Duke of Edinburgh.

Under the Act of Settlement of 1700, which formed part of the Revolution Settlement following the events of 1688 (see p. 3), only Protestant descendants of Princess Sophia, the Electress of Hanover, (a granddaughter of James I of England and VI of Scotland), are eligible to succeed. The order of succession can be altered only by common consent of the countries of the Commonwealth of which the Queen is Sovereign.

Accession

The Sovereign succeeds to the throne as soon as his or her predecessor dies: there is no interregnum. He or she is at once proclaimed at an Accession Council, to which all members of the Privy Council (see p. 128) are summoned. The Lords Spiritual and Temporal (see p. 16), the Lord Mayor and Aldermen and other leading citizens of the City of London, are also invited. The origins of this act of recognition can be traced back to the Anglo-Saxon practice whereby the Witan or Council elected the king from among the members of the royal family.

Coronation

The Sovereign's coronation follows the accession after a convenient interval. The ceremony takes place at Westminster Abbey in London, in the presence of representatives of the Houses of Parliament and of all the great public organisations in Britain. The Prime Ministers and leading members of Commonwealth nations and representatives of other countries also attend.

The Monarch's Role in Government

The Queen personifies the State. In law, she is head of the executive, an integral part of the legislature, head of the judiciary, the commander-in-chief of all the armed forces of the Crown and the 'supreme governor' of the established Church of England. As a result of a long process of evolution during which the Monarchy's absolute power has been progressively reduced (see pp. 2–4), the Queen acts on the advice of her Ministers. Britain is governed by Her Majesty's Government in the name of the Queen.

Within this framework, and in spite of a trend during the past hundred years towards giving powers directly to Ministers, the Queen still takes part in some important acts of government. These include summoning, proroguing (discontinuing until the next session without dissolution) and dissolving Parliament; and giving Royal Assent to Bills passed by Parliament. The Queen also formally appoints many important office holders, including government Ministers, judges, officers in the armed forces, governors, diplomats, bishops and some other senior clergy of the Church of England. She is also involved in pardoning people convicted of crimes; and in conferring peerages, knighthoods and other honours.

One of the Queen's most important functions is appointing the Prime Minister: by convention the Queen invites the leader of the political party which commands a majority in the House of Commons to form a government. In international affairs the Queen, as head of state, has the power to declare war and make peace, to recognise foreign states and governments, to conclude treaties and to annex or cede territory.

With rare exceptions (such as appointing the Prime Minister), acts involving the use of 'royal prerogative' powers are nowadays performed by government Ministers, who are responsible to Parliament and can be questioned about particular policies. Parliamentary authority is not required for the exercise of these prerogative powers, although Parliament may restrict or abolish such rights.

The Queen continues to play a role in the working of government. She holds Privy Council meetings, gives audiences to her Ministers and officials in Britain and overseas, receives accounts of Cabinet decisions, reads dispatches and signs state papers. She must be consulted on every aspect of national life, and must show complete impartiality.

Provision has been made to appoint a regent to perform these royal functions should the Queen be totally incapacitated.

The regent would be the Queen's eldest son, the Prince of Wales, then those, in order of succession to the throne, aged 18 or over. In the event of her partial incapacity or absence abroad, the Queen may delegate certain royal functions to the Counsellors of State (the Duke of Edinburgh, the four adults next in line of succession, and the Queen Mother). However, Counsellors of State may not, for instance, dissolve Parliament (except on the Queen's instructions), nor create peers.

Ceremonial and Royal Visits

Ceremonial has always been associated with the British Monarchy, and, in spite of changes in the outlook of both the Sovereign and the people, many traditional ceremonies continue to take place. Royal marriages and royal funerals are marked by public ceremony and the Sovereign's birthday is officially celebrated in June by Trooping the Colour on Horse Guards Parade. State banquets take place when a foreign monarch or head of state visits Britain; investitures are held at Buckingham Palace and the Palace of Holyroodhouse in Edinburgh to bestow honours; and royal processions add significance to such occasions as a state opening of Parliament.

Each year the Queen and other members of the royal family visit many parts of Britain. They are closely involved in the work of many charities. For example, the Prince of Wales is actively involved in The Prince's Trust, set up to encourage small firms and self-employment in inner cities, while the Princess Royal is President of the Save the Children Fund and takes an active interest in development issues in poorer parts of the world. The Queen pays state visits to foreign governments, accompanied by the Duke of Edinburgh. She also tours the other countries of the

Commonwealth. Other members of the royal family pay official visits overseas, occasionally representing the Queen, or often in connection with an organisation with which they are associated.

Royal Income and Expenditure

Until 1760 the Sovereign had to provide for the payment of all government expenses, including the salaries of officials and the expenses of the royal palaces and households. These were met from hereditary revenues, mainly income from Crown lands, and income from some customs duties, certain taxes and postal revenues granted to the Monarch by Parliament. The income from these sources eventually proved inadequate and in 1760 George III turned over to the Government most of the hereditary revenue. In return he received an annual grant (Civil List) from which he continued to pay the royal expenditure of a personal character, the salaries of government officials, the costs of royal palaces, and certain pensions. The latter charges were removed from the Civil List in 1830.

Present Arrangements

Today the expenditure incurred by the Queen in carrying out her public duties is financed from the Civil List and from government departments—which meet the cost of, for example, the Royal Yacht and the aircraft of No. 32 (The Royal) Squadron. All such expenditure is approved by Parliament. In January 1991 Civil List payments were fixed at £7.9 million a year for ten years. About three-quarters of the Queen's Civil List provision is required to meet the cost of staff. They deal with, among other things, state papers and correspondence, and the organisation of state occasions, visits and other public engagements undertaken by the Queen in Britain and overseas. The Queen's private expenditure as Sovereign is met from the Privy Purse, which is financed mainly from the revenue of the Duchy of Lancaster; her expenditure as a private individual is met from her own personal resources.

Taxation

Under the Civil List Acts, other members of the royal family also receive annual parliamentary allowances to enable them to carry out their public duties. The Prince of Wales, however, receives no such allowance, since as Duke of Cornwall he is entitled to the income of the estate of the Duchy of Cornwall. Each year the Queen refunds the Government for all parliamentary allowances paid to members of the royal family, except the Queen Mother and the Duke of Edinburgh.

Since April 1993 the Queen has voluntarily paid income tax on all her personal income and on that part of the Privy Purse income which is used for private purposes. The Queen also pays tax on any realised capital gains on her private investments and on the private proportion of assets in the Privy Purse. Inheritance tax will not, however, apply to transfers from one sovereign to his or her successor, although any personal bequests other than to the successor will be subject to inheritance tax. In line with these changes the Prince of Wales pays income tax on the income from the Duchy of Cornwall to the extent that it is used for private purposes.

Parliament: the Legislature

Origins of Parliament

The medieval kings were expected to meet all royal expenses, private and public, out of their own revenue. If extra resources were needed for an emergency, such as a war, the Sovereign would seek to persuade his barons, in the Great Council—a gathering of leading men which met several times a year—to grant an aid. During the 13th century several English kings found the private revenues and baronial aids insufficient to meet the expenses of government. They therefore summoned to the Great Council not only the great feudal magnates but also representatives of counties, cities and towns, primarily to get their assent to extraordinary taxation. In this way the Great Council came to include those who were summoned by name (those who, broadly speaking, were to form the House of Lords) and those who were representatives of communities (the commons). The two parts, together with the Sovereign, eventually became known as 'Parliament'. (The term originally meant a meeting for parley or discussion.)[3]

Over the course of time, the commons began to realise the strength of their position. By the middle of the 14th century the formula had appeared which in substance was the same as that used nowadays in voting supplies to the Crown—that is, money to the Government—namely, 'by the Commons with the advice of the Lords Spiritual and Temporal'. In 1407 Henry IV pledged

---

[3]For further details, see *Parliament* (Aspects of Britain: HMSO, 1996).

that henceforth all money grants should be approved by the House of Commons before being considered by the House of Lords.

A similar advance was made in the legislative field. Originally the King's legislation needed only the assent of his councillors. Starting with the right of individual commoners to present petitions, the Commons as a body gained the right to submit collective petitions. Later, during the 15th century, they gained the right to participate in giving their requests—their 'Bills'—the form of law.

The subsequent development of the power of the House of Commons was built upon these foundations. The constitutional developments of the 17th century (see p. 3) led to Parliament securing its position as the supreme legislative authority.

The Powers of Parliament

The three elements which make up Parliament—the Queen, the House of Lords and the elected House of Commons—are constituted on different principles. They meet together only on occasions of symbolic significance such as the State opening of Parliament, when the Commons are summoned by the Queen to the House of Lords. The agreement of all three elements is normally required for legislation, but that of the Queen is given as a matter of course.

Parliament can legislate for Britain as a whole, or for any part of the country. It can also legislate for the Channel Islands (see p. 132) and the Isle of Man (see p. 135), which are Crown dependencies and not part of Britain. They have local legislatures which make laws on island affairs.

As there are no legal restraints imposed by a written constitution, Parliament may legislate as it pleases, subject to Britain's obligations as a member of the European Union. It can make or change any law, and can overturn established conventions or turn them into law. It can even prolong its own life beyond the normal period without consulting the electorate.

In practice, however, Parliament does not assert its supremacy in this way. Its members bear in mind the common law (see p. 102) and normally act in accordance with precedent. The House of Commons is directly responsible to the electorate, and in this century the House of Lords has recognised the supremacy of the elected chamber. The system of party government helps to ensure that Parliament legislates with its responsibility to the electorate in mind.

The Functions of Parliament

The main functions of Parliament are:

—to pass laws;

—to provide, by voting for taxation, the means of carrying on the work of government;

—to scrutinise government policy and administration, including proposals for expenditure; and

—to debate the major issues of the day.

In carrying out these functions Parliament helps to bring the relevant facts and issues before the electorate. By custom, Parliament is also informed before important international treaties and agreements are ratified. The making of treaties is, however, a royal prerogative exercised on the advice of the Government and is not subject to parliamentary approval.

The Meeting of Parliament

A Parliament has a maximum duration of five years, but in practice general elections are usually held before the end of this term. The maximum life has been prolonged by legislation in rare circumstances such as the two World Wars. Parliament is dissolved and writs for a general election are ordered by the Queen on the advice of the Prime Minister.

The life of a Parliament is divided into sessions. Each usually lasts for one year—normally beginning and ending in October or November. There are 'adjournments' at night, at weekends, at Christmas, Easter and the late Spring Bank Holiday, and during a long summer break starting in late July. The average number of 'sitting' days in a session is about 159 in the House of Commons and about 140 in the House of Lords. At the start of each session the Queen's Speech to Parliament outlines the Government's policies and proposed legislative programme. Each session is ended by prorogation. Parliament then 'stands prorogued' for about a week until the new session opens. Prorogation brings to an end nearly all parliamentary business; in particular, public Bills which have not been passed by the end of the session are lost.

The House of Lords

The House of Lords consists of the Lords Spiritual and the Lords Temporal. The Lords Spiritual are the Archbishops of Canterbury and York and 24 senior bishops of the Church of England. The Lords Temporal consist of:

—all hereditary peers of England, Scotland, Great Britain and the United Kingdom (but not peers of Ireland);

—life peers created to assist the House in its judicial duties (Lords of Appeal or 'law lords'); and

—all other life peers.

Hereditary peerages carry a right to sit in the House provided holders establish their claim and are aged 21 years or over. However, anyone succeeding to a peerage may, within 12 months of succession, disclaim that peerage for his or her lifetime.

Peerages, both hereditary and life, are created by the Sovereign on the advice of the Prime Minister. They are usually granted in recognition of service in politics or other walks of life or because one of the political parties wishes to have the recipient in the House of Lords. The House also provides a place in Parliament for people who offer useful advice, but do not wish to be involved in party politics. In addition, senior judges are given life peerages as Lords of Appeal. The House of Lords is the final court of appeal for civil cases in Britain and for criminal cases in England, Wales and Northern Ireland (see p. 105).

In April 1996 there were 1,197 members of the House of Lords, including the two archbishops and 24 bishops. The Lords Temporal consisted of 755 hereditary peers who had succeeded to their titles, 12 hereditary peers who had had their titles conferred on them (including the Prince of Wales), and 404 life peers, of whom 24 were 'law lords'. There were 82 women peers in the House.

Officers of the House of Lords
The House is presided over by the Lord Chancellor, who takes his place on the woolsack as *ex-officio* Speaker of the House. In his absence his place is taken by a deputy. The first of the deputy speakers is the Chairman of Committees, who is appointed at the

beginning of each session and normally chairs Committees of the Whole House and some domestic committees. The Lord Chancellor, the Chairman and Principal Deputy Chairman of Committees are the only Lords who receive salaries as officers of the House.

The Clerk of the Parliaments is responsible for the records of proceedings of the House of Lords and for the text of Acts of Parliament. He is the accounting officer for the costs of the House, and is in charge of the administrative staff of the House, known as the Parliament Office. The Gentleman Usher of the Black Rod, usually known as 'Black Rod', is responsible for security, accommodation and services in the House of Lords' part of the Palace of Westminster.

The House of Commons
The House of Commons is elected by universal adult suffrage and at present consists of 651 Members of Parliament—'MPs'. (See p. 20 for future changes.) In mid-1996 there were 63 women, three Asian and three black MPs. Of the 651 seats, 524 are for England, 38 for Wales, 72 for Scotland, and 17 for Northern Ireland.

General elections are held after a Parliament has been dissolved and a new one summoned by the Queen. When an MP dies or resigns, or is given a peerage, a by-election takes place. Members are paid a basic annual salary (from 1.7.96 to 31.3.97) of £43,000 and an office costs allowance of up to £46,364. There are also a number of other allowances. (For ministers' salaries, see p. 46.)

Officers of the House of Commons
The chief officer of the House of Commons is the Speaker,

elected by MPs to preside over the House. Other officers include the Chairman of Ways and Means and two deputy chairmen, who act as Deputy Speakers. They are elected by the House on the nomination of the Government but are drawn from the Opposition as well as the Government party. They, like the Speaker, neither speak nor vote other than in their official capacity. Responsibility for the administration of the House rests with the House of Commons Commission, a statutory body chaired by the Speaker.

Permanent officers (who are not MPs) include the Clerk of the House of Commons, who is the principal adviser to the Speaker on its privileges and procedures. The Clerk is also accounting officer for the House. The Serjeant-at-Arms, who waits on the Speaker, carries out certain orders of the House. He is also the official housekeeper of the Commons' part of the building, and is responsible for security. Other officers serve the House in the Library, the Department of the Official Report (*Hansard*), the Finance and Administration Department and the Refreshment Department.

Parliamentary Electoral System

For electoral purposes Britain is divided into constituencies, each of which returns one member to the House of Commons.[4] To ensure that constituency electorates are kept roughly equal, four permanent Parliamentary Boundary Commissions, one each for England, Wales, Scotland and Northern Ireland, keep constituencies under review. They recommend any adjustment of seats that may seem necessary in the light of population

---

[4]For further details, see *Parliamentary Elections* (Aspects of Britain: HMSO, 1995).

movements or other changes. Reviews are carried out every eight to 12 years. Elections are by secret ballot.

Planned Changes

The Commissions' last general reviews were approved by Parliament in 1995. As a result of the Commissions' recommendations, the number of parliamentary constituencies—and thus the number of MPs—will increase from 651 to 659.

—England will get an extra five seats (from 524 to 529);

—Wales two (from 38 to 40);

—Northern Ireland one (from 17 to 18);

—The number of seats in Scotland remains unchanged.

The new boundaries will come into effect after the dissolution of Parliament[5] at the next general election.

Voters

British citizens, together with citizens of other Commonwealth countries and citizens of the Irish Republic, resident in Britain, may vote provided they are:

—aged 18 or over;

—included in the annual register of electors for the constituency; and

—not subject to any disqualification.

People not entitled to vote include members of the House of Lords, foreign nationals, some patients detained under mental health legislation, sentenced prisoners and people convicted within the previous five years of corrupt or illegal election practices.

[5]That is, the Parliament elected on 9.4.92.

Members of the armed forces, Crown servants and staff of the British Council employed overseas (together with their wives or husbands if accompanying them) may be registered for an address in the constituency where they would live but for their service. British citizens living abroad may apply to register as electors for a period of 20 years after they have left Britain.

Voting Procedures

Each elector may cast one vote, normally in person at a polling station. Electors whose circumstances on polling day are such that they cannot reasonably be expected to vote in person at their local polling station—for example, electors away on holiday—may apply for an absent vote at a particular election. Electors who are physically incapacitated or unable to vote in person because of the nature of their work, or because they have moved to a new area, may apply for an indefinite absent vote. People entitled to an absent vote may vote by post or by proxy, although postal ballot papers cannot be sent to addresses outside Britain.

Voting is not compulsory; 76.9 per cent of a total electorate of 43.3 million people voted in the general election in April 1992. The simple majority system of voting is used. Candidates are elected if they have more votes than any of the other candidates (although not necessarily an absolute majority over all other candidates).

Candidates

British citizens and citizens of other Commonwealth countries, together with citizens of the Irish Republic, resident in Britain may stand for election as MPs provided they are aged 21 or over and are not disqualified.[6] A candidate's nomination for election must be proposed and seconded by two electors registered as voters in the constituency and signed by eight other electors.

Candidates do not have to be backed by a political party. A candidate must also deposit £500, which is returned if he or she receives 5 per cent or more of the votes cast.

The maximum sum a candidate may spend on a general election campaign is £4,642, plus 3.9 pence for each elector in a borough constituency or 5.2 pence for each elector in a county constituency. Higher limits have been set for by-elections in order to reflect the fact that they are often regarded as tests of national opinion in the period between general elections. A candidate may post an election address to each elector in the constituency, free of charge. All election expenses, apart from the candidate's personal expenses, are subject to the statutory limit.

The Political Party System

The party system, which has existed in one form or another since the 18th century, is an essential element in the working of the constitution.[7] The present system depends upon the existence of organised political parties, each of which presents its policies to the electorate for approval. The parties are not registered nor formally recognised in law, but in practice most candidates in elections—and almost all winning candidates— belong to one of the main parties.

[6]Those disqualified include undischarged bankrupts; people sentenced to more than one year's imprisonment; clergy of the Churches of England, Scotland, Ireland and the Roman Catholic Church; peers; and holders of certain offices listed in the House of Commons Disqualification Act 1975.
[7]For further details, see *Organisation of Political Parties* (Aspects of Britain: HMSO, 1994).

For the last 150 years a predominantly two-party system has existed. Since 1945 either the Conservative Party, whose origins go back to the 18th century, or the Labour Party, which emerged in the last decade of the 19th century, has held power. A new party—the Liberal Democrats—was formed in 1988 when the Liberal Party, which traced its origins to the 18th century, merged with the Social Democratic Party (formed in 1981). Other parties include two nationalist parties, Plaid Cymru (founded in Wales in 1925) and the Scottish National Party (founded in 1934). In Northern Ireland there are a number of parties. They include the Ulster Unionist Party, formed in the early part of this century; the Ulster Democratic Unionist Party, founded in 1971 by a group which broke away from the Ulster Unionists; and the Social Democratic and Labour Party, founded in 1970.

Since 1945 eight general elections have been won by the Conservative Party and six by the Labour Party; the great majority of members of the House of Commons have belonged to one of these two parties. Table 1 shows the results of the last general election.

The party which wins most seats (although not necessarily the most votes) at a general election, or which has the support of a majority of members in the House of Commons, usually forms the Government. By tradition, the leader of the majority party is asked by the Sovereign to form a government. About 100 of its members in the House of Commons and the House of Lords receive ministerial appointments (including appointment to the Cabinet—see p. 46) on the advice of the Prime Minister. The largest minority party becomes the official Opposition, with its own leader and 'shadow cabinet'.

Table 1: Results of the April 1992 General Election

Party	Members elected
Conservative	336
Labour	271
Liberal Democrats	20
Plaid Cymru (Welsh Nationalist)	4
Scottish National	3
Ulster Unionist (Northern Ireland)	9
Ulster Democratic Unionist (Northern Ireland)	3
Ulster Popular Unionist (Northern Ireland)	1
Social Democratic and Labour (Northern Ireland)	4
Total	651

The Party System in Parliament

Leaders of the Government and Opposition sit on the front benches of the Commons with their supporters (the backbenchers) sitting behind them.

Similar arrangements for the parties also apply to the House of Lords; however a significant number of Lords do not wish to be associated with any political party, and sit on the 'crossbenches'. The effectiveness of the party system in Parliament rests largely on the relationship between the Government and the opposition parties. Depending on the relative strengths of the parties in the House of Commons, the Opposition may seek to overthrow the Government by defeating it in a vote on a 'matter of confidence'. In general, however, its aims are to contribute to the formulation of policy and legislation by constructive criticism; to oppose government proposals it considers objectionable; to seek amendments to Government Bills; and to put forward its own policies in order to improve its chances of winning the next general election.

The detailed arrangements of government business are settled, under the direction of the Prime Minister and the Leaders of the two Houses, by the Government Chief Whips of each House in consultation with the Opposition Chief Whips. The Chief Whips together constitute the 'usual channels' often referred to when the question of finding time for a particular item of business is discussed. The Leaders of the two Houses are responsible for enabling the Houses to debate matters about which they are concerned.

Outside Parliament, party control is exercised by the national and local organisations. Inside, it is exercised by the Chief Whips and their assistants, who are chosen within the party. Their duties include keeping members informed of forthcoming parliamentary business, maintaining the party's voting strength by ensuring members attend important debates, and passing on to the party leadership the opinions of backbench members. Party discipline tends to be less strong in the Lords than in the Commons, since Lords have less hope of high office and no need of party support in elections.

Financial Assistance to Parties
Annual assistance from public funds helps opposition parties carry out their parliamentary work at Westminster. It is limited to parties which had at least two members elected at the previous general election or one member elected and a minimum of 150,000 votes cast.

The amount for the period 1 April 1996 to 31 March 1997 is £3,743.33 for every seat won, plus £7.48 for every 200 votes. The amounts are increased annually by reference to the Retail Prices Index.

Parliamentary Procedure

Parliamentary procedure is based on custom and precedent, partly codified by each House in its Standing Orders. The system of debate is similar in both Houses. Every subject starts off as a proposal or 'motion' by a member. After debate, in which each member may speak once only, the Speaker or Chairman 'puts the question' whether to agree with the motion or not. The question may be decided without voting, or by a simple majority vote. The main difference of procedure between the two Houses is that the Speaker or Chairman in the Lords has no powers of order; instead such matters are decided by the general feeling of the House. In the Commons the Speaker has full authority to enforce the rules of the House.

The Speaker supervises voting in the Commons and announces the final result. In a tied vote the Speaker gives a casting vote. The voting procedure in the House of Lords is broadly similar, although the Lord Chancellor does not have a casting vote.

Financial Interests

The Commons has a public register of MPs' financial (and some non-financial) interests. Members with a financial interest must declare it when speaking in the House or in Committee and must indicate it when giving notice of a question or motion. In

November 1995 the House agreed to prohibit any form of advocacy in the House by an MP on behalf of a body with which he or she has a paid agreement.

In November 1995 the House of Lords passed a Resolution revising the guidance on declaration of interests and establishing a *Register of Lords' Interests*, on lines similar to that for MPs. The first *Register* was published in February 1996 and is open to public inspection.

Parliamentary Commissioner for Standards

Following recommendations of the Committee on Standards in Public Life (the Nolan Committee—see p. 58), the new post of Parliamentary Commissioner for Standards was created in November 1995. The Commissioner can advise MPs on matters of standards and conduct a preliminary investigation into complaints about alleged breaches of the rules. The Commissioner reports to the House of Commons Select Committee on Standards and Privileges.

Public Access to Parliamentary Proceedings

Proceedings of both Houses are normally public. The minutes and speeches (transcribed verbatim in *Hansard*, the official report) are published daily.

The records of the Lords from 1497 and of the Commons from 1547, are available to the public through the House of Lords Record Office.

The proceedings of both Houses of Parliament may be broadcast on television and radio, either live or, more usually, in recorded or edited form. Complete coverage is available on cable television.

The Law-making Process

Statute law consists of Acts of Parliament and delegated legislation made by Ministers under powers given to them by Act (see p. 32). While the law undergoes constant refinement in the courts (see p. 102), changes to statute law are made by Parliament.

Draft laws take the form of parliamentary Bills. Proposals for legislation affecting the powers of particular bodies (such as local authorities) or the rights of individuals (such as certain proposals relating to railways, roads and harbours) are known as Private Bills, and are subject to a special form of parliamentary procedure. Bills which change the general law and which constitute the more significant part of the parliamentary legislative process are Public Bills.

Public Bills can be introduced into either House, by a government minister or by an ordinary ('private' or 'backbench') member. Most Public Bills that become Acts of Parliament are introduced by a government minister and are known as 'Government Bills'. Bills introduced by other members of Parliament are known as 'Private Members' Bills'.

The main Bills which constitute the Government's legislative programme are announced in the Queen's Speech at the State opening of Parliament, which usually takes place in November, and the Bills themselves are introduced into one or other of the Houses over the succeeding weeks.

Before a Government Bill is drafted, there may be consultation with professional bodies, voluntary organisations and other agencies interested in the subject, and interest and pressure groups which seek to promote specific causes. Proposals for legislative changes are sometimes set out in government 'White Papers' which may be debated in Parliament before a Bill is introduced. From time to time, consultation papers, sometimes called 'Green Papers', set out government proposals which are still taking shape and seek comments from the public.

Private Members' Bills

Early in each session backbench members of the Commons ballot (draw lots) for the opportunity to introduce a Bill on one of the Fridays during the session on which such Bills have precedence over government business. The first 20 Members whose names are drawn win this privilege, but it does not guarantee that their Bills will pass into law. Members may also present a Bill on any day without debate, and on most Tuesdays and Wednesdays on which the Commons is sitting there is also an opportunity to seek leave to present a Bill under the 'ten-minute rule'. This provides an opportunity for a brief speech by the Member proposing the Bill (and by one who opposes it).

Few of these Bills make further progress or receive any debate, but in most sessions a few do become law. Recent examples include the Marriage Act 1994, the Building Societies (Joint Account Holders) Act 1995 and the Wild Mammals (Protection) Act 1996. Private Members' Bills do not often call for the expenditure of public money; but if they do they cannot proceed to committee stage unless the Government decides to provide the necessary money. Peers may introduce Private Members' Bills in the House of Lords at any time. A Private Member's Bill passed by either House will not proceed in the other House unless taken up by a member of that House.

Passage of Public Bills

Public Bills must normally be passed by both Houses. Bills relating mainly to financial matters are almost invariably introduced in the Commons. Under the provisions of the Parliament Acts 1911 and 1949, the powers of the Lords in relation to 'money Bills', are very restricted. The Parliament Acts also provide for a Bill to be passed by the Commons without consent of the Lords in certain (very rare) circumstances.

The process of passing a Public Bill is similar in each House. On presentation the Bill is considered, without debate, to have been read for a first time and is printed (although a substantial number of Private Members' Bills are never printed.) After an interval, which may be between one day and several weeks, a Government Bill will receive its second reading debate, during which the general principles of the Bill are discussed. If it obtains a second reading in the Commons, a Bill will normally be committed to a standing committee (see p. 34) for detailed examination and amendment. In the Lords, the committee stage usually takes place on the floor of the House, and this procedure may also be followed in the Commons if that House so decides (usually in cases where there is a need to pass the Bill quickly or where it raises matters of constitutional importance.) The Commons may also decide to divide the committee stage of a Bill between a standing committee and a committee of the whole House (which is commonly the case with the annual Finance Bill).

The committee stage is followed by the report stage ('consideration') on the floor of the House, during which further amendments may be made. In the Commons, this is usually followed immediately by the third reading debate, where the Bill is reviewed in its final form. In the Lords, a Bill may be further amended at third reading.

After passing its third reading in one House, a Bill is sent to the other House, where it passes through all its stages once more, and where it is, more often than not, further amended. Amendments made by the second House must be agreed by the first, or a compromise reached, before a Bill can go for Royal Assent.

In the Commons the House may vote to limit the time available for consideration of a Bill. This is done by passing a 'timetable' motion proposed by the Government, commonly referred to as a 'guillotine'.

There are special procedures for Public Bills which consolidate existing legislation or which enact private legislation relating to Scotland.

Royal Assent

When a Bill has passed through all its parliamentary stages, it is sent to the Queen for Royal Assent, after which it is part of the law of the land and known as an Act of Parliament. The Royal Assent has not been refused since 1707.

Limitations on the Power of the Lords

Most Government Bills introduced and passed in the Lords pass through the Commons without difficulty, but a Lords Bill which is unacceptable to the Commons will not become law. The Lords, on the other hand, do not generally prevent Bills insisted upon by the Commons from becoming law, though they will often amend them and return them for further consideration by the Commons.

By convention, the Lords pass Bills authorising taxation or national expenditure without amendment. Under the Parliament

Acts 1911 and 1949, a Bill that deals only with taxation or expenditure must become law within one month of being sent to the Lords, whether or not they agree to it, unless the Commons directs otherwise. If no agreement is reached between the two Houses on a non-financial Commons Bill the Lords can delay the Bill for a period which, in practice, amounts to at least 13 months. Following this the Bill may be submitted to the Queen for Royal Assent, provided it has been passed a second time by the Commons. The Parliament Acts make one important exception: any Bill to lengthen the life of a Parliament requires the full assent of both Houses in the normal way.

The limits to the power of the Lords, contained in the Parliament Acts, are based on the belief that nowadays the main legislative function of the non-elected House is to act as a chamber of revision, complementing but not rivalling the elected House.

Delegated Legislation

In order to reduce unnecessary pressure on parliamentary time, primary legislation often gives Ministers or other authorities the power to regulate administrative details by means of secondary or 'delegated' legislation. To minimise any risk that delegating powers to the executive might undermine the authority of Parliament, such powers are normally delegated only to authorities directly accountable to Parliament. Moreover, Acts of Parliament which delegate such powers usually provide for some measure of direct parliamentary control over proposed delegated legislation, by giving Parliament the opportunity to affirm or annul it. Certain Acts also require that organisations affected must be consulted before rules and orders can be made.

A joint committee of both Houses reports on the technical propriety of all these 'statutory instruments'. One specific type of statutory instrument—known as a deregulation order—is subject to a different committee procedure in each House. In order to save time on the floor of the House, the Commons uses standing committees to debate the merits of instruments; actual decisions are taken by the House as a whole. The House of Lords has appointed a delegated powers scrutiny committee which examines the appropriateness of the powers to make secondary legislation in Bills as they come before the House.

Private and Hybrid Bills

Private Bills are promoted by people or organisations outside Parliament (often local authorities) to give them special legal powers. They go through a similar procedure to Public Bills, but most of the work is done in committee, where procedures follow a semi-judicial pattern. Hybrid Bills are Public Bills which may affect private rights. As with Private Bills, the passage of Hybrid Bills through Parliament is governed by special procedures which allow those affected to put their case.

Parliamentary Committees

Committees of the Whole House

Either House may pass a resolution setting itself up as a Committee of the whole House to consider Bills in detail after their second reading. This permits unrestricted discussion: the general rule that an MP or Lord may speak only once on each motion does not apply in committee.

Standing Committees

House of Commons standing committees debate and consider public Bills at the committee stage. The committee considers the Bill clause by clause, and may amend it before reporting it back to the House. Ordinary standing committees do not have names but are referred to simply as Standing Committee A, B, C, and so on; a new set of members is appointed to them to consider each Bill. Each committee has between 16 and 50 members, with a party balance reflecting as far as possible that in the House as a whole.

The standing committees include two Scottish standing committees, and the Scottish, Welsh and Northern Ireland Grand Committees.

The Scottish Grand Committee comprises all 72 Scottish members (and may be convened anywhere in Scotland as well as Westminster). It may consider the principles of Scottish Bills referred to it at second reading stage and at third reading stage Ministers not appointed to the Committee may also move motions. It also debates Scottish public expenditure estimates and other matters concerning Scotland. Since July 1994 these have included questions tabled for oral answer, ministerial statements and other debates in addition to statutory instruments referred to it.

The Welsh Grand Committee, with all 38 Welsh members and up to five others, considers Bills referred to it at second reading stage, questions tabled for oral answer, ministerial statements, and other matters. The Northern Ireland Grand Committee debates matters relating specifically to Northern Ireland. It includes all 17 Northern Ireland members and up to 25 others.

There are also standing committees to debate proposed

European legislation, and to scrutinise statutory instruments made by the Government.

In the Lords, various sorts of committees on Bills may be used instead of, or as well as, a Committee of the Whole House. They include Public Bill Committees, Special Public Bill Committees, Committees off the Floor of the House and Scottish Public Bill Committees.

Select Committees

Select committees are appointed for a particular task, generally one of inquiry, investigation and scrutiny. They report their conclusions and recommendations to the House as a whole; in many cases their recommendations invite a response from the Government, which is also reported to the House. A select committee may be appointed for a Parliament, or for a session, or for as long as it takes to complete its task. To help Parliament with the control of the executive by examining aspects of public policy, expenditure and administration, 17 committees have been established by the House of Commons to examine the work of the main government departments and their associated public bodies. The Foreign Affairs Select Committee, for example, 'shadows' the work of the Foreign & Commonwealth Office. The committees are constituted on a basis which is in approximate proportion to party strength in the House.

Other regular Commons select committees include those on Public Accounts, Standards and Privileges, European Legislation, and the Parliamentary Commissioner for Administration (the 'Parliamentary Ombudsman'—see p. 40). Since March 1995 there has also been a Deregulation Committee, which examines proposals and draft orders to be made under the Deregulation and Contracting Out Act 1994. Domestic select committees also cover the internal workings of Parliament.

In their examination of government policies, expenditure and administration, committees may question ministers, civil servants and interested bodies and individuals. Through hearings and published reports, they bring before Parliament and the public an extensive body of fact and informed opinion on many issues, and build up considerable expertise in their subjects of inquiry.

In the House of Lords, besides the Appeal and Appellate Committees, in which the bulk of the House's judicial work is transacted, there are two major select committees (along with several sub-committees), on the European Community and on Science and Technology. *Ad hoc* committees may also be set up to consider particular issues (or sometimes, a particular Bill), and 'domestic' committees—as in the Commons—cover the internal workings of the House.

Joint Committees
Joint committees, with a membership drawn from both Houses, are appointed in each session to deal with Consolidation Bills and delegated legislation. The two Houses may also agree to set up joint select committees on other subjects.

Party Committees
In addition to the official committees of the two Houses there are several unofficial party organisations or committees. The Conservative and Unionist Members' Committee (the 1922 Committee) consists of the backbench membership of the party in the House of Commons. When the Conservative Party is in office, ministers attend its meetings by invitation and not by

right. When the party is in opposition, the whole membership of the party may attend meetings. The leader then appoints a consultative committee, which acts as the party's 'shadow cabinet'.

The Parliamentary Labour Party comprises all members of the party in both Houses. When the Labour Party is in office, a parliamentary committee, half of whose members are elected and half of whom are government representatives, acts as a channel of communication between the Government and its backbenchers in both Houses. When the party is in opposition, the Parliamentary Labour Party is organised under the direction of an elected parliamentary committee, which acts as the 'shadow cabinet'.

Other Forms of Parliamentary Control

In addition to the system of scrutiny by select committees, both Houses offer a number of opportunities for the examination of government policy by both the Opposition and the Government's own backbenchers. In the House of Commons these include:

—Question Time, when for 55 minutes on Monday, Tuesday, Wednesday and Thursday, Ministers answer MPs' questions. The Prime Minister's Question Time is every Tuesday and Thursday when the House is sitting. Parliamentary questions are one means of seeking information about the Government's intentions. They are also a way of raising grievances brought to MPs' notice by constituents. MPs may also put questions to Ministers for written answer; the questions and answers are published in *Hansard*. There are some 50,000 questions every year.

—Adjournment debates, when MPs use motions for the adjournment of the House to raise constituency cases or matters of public concern. There is a half-hour adjournment period at the end of the business of the day, while immediately before the adjournment for each recess (Parliament's Christmas, Easter, Whitsun and summer breaks) three hours is spent discussing issues raised by private members.

In addition, an MP wishing to discuss a 'specific and important matter that should have urgent consideration' may, at the end of Question Time, seek leave to move the adjournment of the House. On the very few occasions when leave is obtained, the matter is debated for three hours in what is known as an emergency debate, usually on the following day.

—Early day motions (EDMs) provide a further opportunity for backbench MPs to express their views on particular issues. A number of EDMs are tabled each sitting day; they are very rarely debated but can be useful in gauging the degree of support for the issue by the number of signatures of other MPs which the motion attracts.

—The 20 Opposition days each session, when the Opposition can choose subjects for debate. Of these days, 17 are at the disposal of the Leader of the Opposition and three at the disposal of the second largest opposition party.

—Debates on three days in each session on details of proposed government expenditure, chosen by the Liaison Committee.

Procedural opportunities for criticism of the Government also arise during the debate on the Queen's Speech at the beginning of each session; during debates on motions of censure for which the Government provides time; and during debates on the

Government's legislative and other proposals.

House of Lords
Similar opportunities for criticism and examination of government policy are provided in the House of Lords at daily Question Time, during debates and by means of questions for written answer.

Control of Finances
The main responsibilities of Parliament, and more particularly of the House of Commons, in overseeing the revenue of the State and public expenditure, are to authorise the raising of taxes and duties, and the various objects of expenditure and the sum to be spent on each. It also has to satisfy itself that the sums granted are spent only for the purposes which Parliament intended. No payment out of the central government's public funds can be made and no taxation or loans authorised, except by Act of Parliament. However, limited interim payments can be made from the Contingencies Fund.

The Finance Act is the most important of the annual statutes, and authorises the raising of revenue. The legislation is based on the Chancellor of the Exchequer's Budget statement. It includes a review of the public finances of the previous year, and proposals for future expenditure. Scrutiny of public expenditure is carried out by House of Commons select committees (see p. 35).

European Union Affairs
To keep the two Houses informed of European Union (EU) developments, and to enable them to scrutinise and debate Union policies and proposals, there is a select committee in each

House and two Commons standing committees debate specific European legislative proposals. Ministers also make regular statements about Union business.

The Commons' Ability to Force the Government to Resign
The final control is the ability of the House of Commons to force the Government to resign by passing a resolution of 'no confidence'. The Government must also resign if the House rejects a proposal which the Government considers so vital to its policy that it has declared it a 'matter of confidence' or if the House refuses to vote the money required for the public service.

Parliamentary Commissioner for Administration
The Parliamentary Ombudsman—officially known as the Parliamentary Commissioner for Administration—investigates complaints from members of the public (referred through MPs) alleging that they have suffered injustice arising from maladministration. The Ombudsman is independent of government and reports to a Select Committee of the House of Commons. The Ombudsman's jurisdiction covers central government departments and a large number of non-departmental public bodies. He cannot investigate complaints about government policy, the content of legislation or relations with other countries.

In making his investigations, the Commissioner has access to all departmental papers, and has powers to summon those from whom he wishes to take evidence. When an investigation is completed, he sends a report with his findings to the MP who referred the complaint (with a copy report for the complainant). In reports of justified cases, the Ombudsman normally recommends that the department provides redress (which can include a financial remedy for the complainant in appropriate cases). There is no appeal against the Ombudsman's decision. He submits an annual report to Parliament, and also publishes selected cases three times a year.

In 1995 the Ombudsman received 1,706 new complaints. He completed 245 investigations; of these he found 236 wholly or partly justified and 9 unjustified.

The Parliamentary Ombudsman also monitors the Code of Practice on Access to Official Information (see p. 57).

Parliamentary Privilege

Each House of Parliament has certain rights and immunities to protect it from obstruction in carrying out its duties. The rights apply collectively to each House and to its staff and individually to each member.

For the Commons the Speaker formally claims from the Queen 'their ancient and undoubted rights and privileges' at the beginning of each Parliament. These include freedom of speech; first call on the attendance of its members, who are therefore free from arrest in civil actions and exempt from serving on juries, or being compelled to attend court as witnesses; and the right of access to the Crown, which is a collective privilege of the House. Further privileges include the rights of the House to control its own proceedings (so that it is able, for instance, to exclude 'strangers'[8] if it wishes); to decide upon legal disqualifications for membership and to declare a seat vacant on such grounds; and to punish for breach of its privileges and for contempt. Parliament has the right to punish anybody, inside or outside the House,

[8]All those who are not members or officials of either House.

who commits a breach of privilege—that is, offends against the rights of the House.

The privileges of the House of Lords are broadly similar to those of the House of Commons.

The Executive

Her Majesty's Government

Composition of the Government

Her Majesty's Government is the body of ministers responsible for the conduct of national affairs. The Prime Minister is appointed by the Queen, and all other Ministers are appointed by the Queen on the recommendation of the Prime Minister. Most Ministers are members of the House of Commons, although the Government is also fully represented by Ministers in the House of Lords. The Lord Chancellor is always a member of the Lords.

The composition of governments can vary both in the number of Ministers and in the titles of some offices. New ministerial offices may be created, others may be abolished, and functions may be transferred from one Minister to another.

Prime Minister

The Prime Minister is also, by tradition, First Lord of the Treasury and Minister for the Civil Service. The head of the Government became known as the Prime Minister during the 18th century (see p. 4). The Prime Minister's unique position of authority derives from majority support in the House of Commons and from the power to appoint and dismiss Ministers. By modern convention, the Prime Minister always sits in the House of Commons.

The Prime Minister presides over the Cabinet, is responsible for the allocation of functions among Ministers and informs the Queen at regular meetings of the general business of the Government.

The Prime Minister's other responsibilities include recommending a number of appointments to the Queen. These include:

— Church of England archbishops, bishops and deans and some 200 clergy in Crown 'livings';

— Senior judges, such as the Lord Chief Justice;

— Privy Counsellors (see p. 128); and

— Lord Lieutenants.

They also include certain civil appointments, such as Lord High Commissioner to the General Assembly of the Church of Scotland, Poet Laureate, Constable of the Tower, and some university posts; and appointments to various public boards and institutions, such as the BBC (British Broadcasting Corporation), as well as various royal and statutory commissions. Recommendations are likewise made for the award of many civil honours and distinctions and of Civil List pensions (to people who have achieved eminence in science and the arts and are in financial need). The Prime Minister also selects the trustees of certain national museums and institutions.

The Prime Minister's Office at 10 Downing Street (the official residence in central London) has a staff of civil servants who assist the Prime Minister. The Prime Minister may also appoint special advisers to the Office from time to time to assist in the formation of policies.

Departmental Ministers

Ministers in charge of government departments are usually in the Cabinet; they are known as 'Secretary of State' or 'Minister', or may have a special title, as in the case of the Chancellor of the Exchequer.

Non-departmental Ministers

The holders of various traditional offices, namely the Lord President of the Council, the Chancellor of the Duchy of Lancaster, the Lord Privy Seal, the Paymaster General and, from time to time, Ministers without Portfolio, may have few or no departmental duties. They are thus available to perform any duties the Prime Minister may wish to give them. In the present administration, for example, the Lord President of the Council is leader of the House of Commons and the Chancellor of the Duchy of Lancaster is Minister for the Public Service.

Lord Chancellor and Law Officers

The Lord Chancellor holds a special position, as both a Minister with departmental functions and the head of the judiciary (see p. 104). The four Law Officers of the Crown are: for England and Wales, the Attorney General and the Solicitor General; and for Scotland, the Lord Advocate and the Solicitor General for Scotland.

Ministers of State and Junior Ministers

Ministers of State usually work with Ministers in charge of departments. They normally have specific responsibilities, and are sometimes given titles which reflect these functions. More than one may work in a department. A Minister of State may be given a seat in the Cabinet and be paid accordingly.

Junior Ministers (generally Parliamentary Under-Secretaries

of State) share in parliamentary and departmental duties. They may also be given responsibility, directly under the departmental Minister, for specific aspects of the department's work.

Ministerial Salaries

From 24.7.96 to the next Parliament[9] the salaries of ministers in the House of Commons range from £66,623 a year for junior ministers to £86,991 for Cabinet ministers. In the House of Lords salaries range from £43,632 for junior ministers to £58,876 for Cabinet ministers. The Prime Minister receives £101,557 and the Lord Chancellor £133,406.

Ministers in the Commons, including the Prime Minister, receive a full parliamentary salary of £43,000 a year (which is included in the above figures) in recognition of their constituency responsibilities and can claim the other allowances which are paid to all MPs (see p. 18).

The Leader of the Opposition in the Commons is entitled to a salary of £83,332 (including the full parliamentary salary)[10]; three Opposition Whips in the Commons and the Opposition Leader and Chief Whip in the Lords also receive salaries.

The Cabinet

The Cabinet is composed of about 20 Ministers (the number can vary) chosen by the Prime Minister and may include departmental and non-departmental Ministers.

The functions of the Cabinet are to initiate and decide on policy, the supreme control of government and the co-ordination

[9]That is, the Parliament following that elected on 9.4.92.
[10]Since 1989 the Leader of the Opposition has declined the pay increases awarded; he draws instead a salary of £67,456.

of government departments. The exercise of these functions is vitally affected by the fact that the Cabinet is a group of party representatives, depending upon majority support in the House of Commons.

Cabinet Meetings

The Cabinet meets in private and its proceedings are confidential. Its members are bound by their oath as Privy Counsellors not to disclose information about its proceedings, although after 30 years Cabinet papers may be made available for inspection in the Public Record Office at Kew, Surrey.

Normally the Cabinet meets for a few hours each week during parliamentary sittings, and rather less often when Parliament is not sitting. To keep its workload within manageable limits, a great deal of work is carried on through the committee system. This involves referring issues either to a standing Cabinet committee or to an *ad hoc* committee composed of the Ministers directly concerned. The committee then considers the matter in detail and either disposes of it or reports upon it to the Cabinet with recommendations for action.

There are standing committees dealing with defence and overseas policy, economic and domestic policy, and legislation. The membership and terms of reference of all ministerial Cabinet committees are published by the Cabinet Office. Where appropriate, the Secretary of the Cabinet and other senior officials of the Cabinet Office attend meetings of the Cabinet and its committees.

Diaries published by several former Ministers have given the public insight into Cabinet procedures in recent times.

The Cabinet Office

The Cabinet Office is headed by the Secretary of the Cabinet (a civil servant who is also Head of the Home Civil Service), under the direction of the Prime Minister. It comprises the Cabinet Secretariat and the Office of Public Service (OPS).

The Cabinet Secretariat serves Ministers collectively in the conduct of Cabinet business, and in the co-ordination of policy at the highest level.

The Chancellor of the Duchy of Lancaster is in charge of the OPS and is a member of the Cabinet. The OPS is responsible for:

—raising the standard of public services across the public sector through the Citizen's Charter programme (see p. 53);

—promoting the Government's policies on competitiveness and deregulation;

—increasing the openness of central government; and

—improving the effectiveness and efficiency of central government, through, among other things, the establishment of executive agencies and the market-testing programme (see p. 62–3).

The Historical and Records Section is responsible for Official Histories and managing Cabinet Office records.

Ministerial Responsibility

'Ministerial responsibility' refers both to the collective responsibility for government policy and actions, which Ministers share, and to Ministers' individual responsibility for their departments' work.

The doctrine of collective responsibility means that the Cabinet acts unanimously even when Cabinet Ministers do not all agree on a subject. The policy of departmental Ministers must be consistent with the policy of the Government as a whole. Once the Government's policy on a matter has been decided, each Minister is expected to support it or resign. On rare occasions, Ministers have been allowed free votes in Parliament on government policies involving important issues of principle. In February 1994, for example, free votes were allowed on lowering the age of consent for homosexuals from 21 to 18.

The individual responsibility of Ministers for the work of their departments means that they are answerable to Parliament for all their departments' activities. They bear the consequences of any failure in administration, any injustice to an individual or any aspect of policy which may be criticised in Parliament, whether personally responsible or not. Since most Ministers are members of the House of Commons, they must answer questions and defend themselves against criticism in person. Departmental Ministers in the House of Lords are represented in the Commons by someone qualified to speak on their behalf, usually a junior Minister.

Departmental Ministers normally decide all matters within their responsibility. However, on important political matters they usually consult their colleagues collectively, either through the Cabinet or through a Cabinet committee. A decision by a departmental Minister binds the Government as a whole.

On assuming office, Ministers must resign directorships in private and public companies, and must ensure that there is no conflict between their public duties and private interests.

Government Departments and Agencies

Government departments and their agencies, staffed by politically impartial civil servants, are the main instruments for implementing government policy when Parliament has passed the necessary legislation, and for advising Ministers. They often work alongside local authorities, statutory boards, and government-sponsored organisations operating under various degrees of government control.

A change of government does not necessarily affect the number or general functions of government departments, although major changes in policy may be accompanied by organisational changes.

The work of some departments (for instance, the Ministry of Defence) covers Britain as a whole. Other departments, such as the Department of Social Security, cover England, Wales and Scotland, but not Northern Ireland. Others, such as the Department of the Environment, are mainly concerned with affairs in England. Some departments, such as the Department of Trade and Industry, maintain a regional organisation, and some which have direct contact with the public throughout the country (for example, the Department of Social Security) also have local offices.

Departments are usually headed by Ministers. In some departments the head is a permanent official, and Ministers with other duties are responsible for them to Parliament. For instance, Ministers in the Treasury are responsible for HM Customs and Excise, the Inland Revenue, the National Investment and Loans Office and a number of other departments as well as executive agencies such as the Royal Mint. Departments generally receive their funds directly out of money provided by Parliament and are staffed by members of the Civil Service.

The functions of the main government departments are set

out in Appendix 1 (see p. 112). The work of the Welsh, Scottish and Northern Ireland Offices is covered on pp. 84–5, 86–9 and 94–7.

Non-departmental Public Bodies

Non-departmental public bodies (NDPBs) are bodies which have a role in the process of national government but are not government departments nor parts of a department. There are three kinds: executive bodies, advisory bodies and tribunals. Tribunals are a specialised group of bodies whose functions are essentially judicial (see p. 107).

The function of NDPBs is regularly reviewed in a continuous programme. Once they are no longer needed in their existing form, the bodies are abolished, merged or privatised. The number of NDPBs decreased from 2,167 in 1979 to 1,227 in 1995, a reduction of 43 per cent. During the same period the number of staff they employed decreased from 217,000 to 109,200—a reduction of 45 per cent. (See p. 59 for government plans to increase the public accountability of NDPBs.)

Executive Bodies
Executive bodies normally employ their own staff and have their own budget. They are public organisations whose duties include executive, administrative, regulatory or commercial functions. They normally operate within broad policy guidelines set by departmental Ministers but are in varying degrees independent of government in carrying out their day-to-day responsibilities. Examples include the Commission for Racial Equality, the Police Complaints Authority, and the Public Health Laboratory Service.

Advisory Bodies

Many government departments are assisted by advisory councils or committees which undertake research and collect information, mainly to give Ministers access to informed opinion before they come to a decision involving a legislative or executive act. In some cases a Minister must consult a standing committee, but advisory bodies are usually appointed at the discretion of the Minister. Examples include the British Overseas Trade Board and the Farm Animal Welfare Council.

The membership of the advisory councils and committees varies according to the nature of the work involved, but normally includes representatives of the relevant interests and professions.

In addition to standing advisory bodies, there are committees set up by government to examine specific matters and make recommendations. For example, the Committee on Standards in Public Life (the Nolan Committee—see p. 58) was set up in 1994, reporting directly to the Prime Minister.

For certain important inquiries, Royal Commissions, whose members are chosen for their wide experience, may be appointed. Royal Commissions examine evidence from government departments, interested organisations and individuals, and submit recommendations. Some prepare regular reports. Examples include: the standing Royal Commission on Environmental Pollution, set up in 1970; and the Royal Commission on Criminal Justice, which was set up in 1991 and reported in 1993. Royal Commissions are often referred to by the names of the people who have chaired them.

Inquiries may also be undertaken by departmental committees.

Government Information Services

Each of the main government departments has its own information division, public relations branch or news department. These are normally staffed by professional information officers responsible for communicating their department's activities to the news media and the public (sometimes using publicity services provided by the Central Office of Information—see p. 126). They also advise their departments on the public's reaction.

The Lobby

As press adviser to the Prime Minister, the Prime Minister's Press Secretary and other staff in the Prime Minister's Press Office have direct contact with the parliamentary press through regular meetings with the Lobby correspondents. The Lobby correspondents are a group of political correspondents who have the special privilege of access to the Lobby of the House of Commons, where they can talk privately to government Ministers and other members of the House. The Prime Minister's Press Office is the accepted channel through which information about parliamentary business is passed to the media.

Improving Public Services: the Citizen's Charter

The Citizen's Charter was launched by the Prime Minister in 1991 as a ten-year programme to raise the standard of public services and make them more responsive to the needs and wishes of their users. It is closely linked to other reforms, including the Next Steps programme, efficiency measures and the Government's contracting out and market-testing programmes (see p. 63).

The Charter applies to all public services, at both national and local level, and to the services delivered by the regulated utilities in the absence of a genuinely competitive market.

National charters have set a minimum framework of standards for a range of public services. There are now 40 main charters, covering all the key public services, setting out the standards of service people can expect to receive. There are also many thousands of local charters covering the providers of local services, such as individual GP practices, police forces and fire services, often developed and improved after consultation with local users.

The Principles of Public Service
The Charter sets out a number of key principles which users of services are entitled to expect:

—*Standards:* setting, monitoring and publishing explicit standards for the services that individual users can reasonably expect. Publication of actual performance against these standards;

—*Information and Openness:* full and accurate information readily available in plain language about how public services are run, their cost and performance, and who is in charge;

—*Choice and Consultation:* regular and systematic consultation with those who use services. Users' views about services, and their priorities for improving them, should be taken into account in final decisions about standards;

—*Courtesy and Helpfulness:* courteous and helpful service from public servants who will normally wear name badges. Services available equally to all who are entitled to them and run to suit their convenience;

—*Putting Things Right:* if things go wrong, an apology, a full explanation and a swift and effective remedy should be given. Well publicised and easy-to-use complaints procedures, with independent review wherever possible, should be available;

—*Value for Money:* efficient and economical delivery of public services within the resources the nation can afford, and independent validation of performance against standards.

Implementing the Charter

A Cabinet Minister, the Chancellor of the Duchy of Lancaster, is responsible for the Citizen's Charter programme. The Citizen's Charter Unit, based in the OPS (see p. 48), co-ordinates activity on the Charter programme and reports on progress. It supports the Prime Minister's Panel of Advisers, which provides independent advice to government on the application, implementation and development of the Charter programme.

Executive agencies (see p. 62) are expected to comply fully with the principles of the Citizen's Charter, and the pay of agency chief executives is normally directly related to their agency's performance. Performance-related pay is being introduced throughout the public service.

Progress on the Charter

Projects to ensure that public service managers understand the benefits of the Charter programme and that users are aware of the standards of service they can expect to receive include:

—*Charter Mark Awards:* the Charter Mark Scheme was introduced in 1992 to reward excellence in the delivery of public services. The scheme is open to all public sector organisations that deliver a service direct to the public and to privatised utilities. Awards are made for three years. To win, applicants must meet nine assessment criteria such as value for money, measurable improvements in the quality of service, and choice and consultation. Trained Charter Mark assessors are drawn from all parts of the public and private sectors. Final decisions are taken by an independent judging panel. In 1995 a record number of 740 applications were received and 224 awards were made. Winners came from all parts of the public sector throughout Britain. They included: the St James's University Hospital Liver Unit (Leeds), Employment Service (Inverness), Merthyr Tydfil Libraries, the UK Passport Agency (London) and Northern Ireland Housing Executive (Lisburn).

In 1995, for the first time, members of the public were invited to nominate services for a Charter Mark. Over 4,000 nominations were received for more than 2,000 organisations.

—*Charter Quality Networks:* the Charter Unit has helped to set up a number of networks of groups of managers of public services to meet locally to exchange ideas on customer service and quality issues and share best practice. There are 24 Quality Networks around Britain, with over 1,000 members. The networks aim to help break down boundaries between public service organisations and encourage problem-sharing and solving. The Charter Unit continues to support networks and involve network leaders in developments in the Charter programmes.

—*Charter Quality Seminars and Workshops:* the Charter Unit runs and arranges a number of seminars and workshops to allow local public services managers and consumer groups to share experiences in delivering a high-quality service to their customers. Seminars have been held for local authorities; secondary, further and higher education; those involved in community care; services to road users; services in rural areas; effective complaints handling; and one-stop services.

Charter News is a free quarterly magazine distributed to managers throughout the public services. It helps to spread best practice and raise awareness of the Charter programme.

Open Government

In line with Citizen's Charter principles of increased openness and accountability of public administration, the Government introduced the Code of Practice on Access to Government Information in 1994.[11] Under the Code, government departments and bodies within the jurisdiction of the Parliamentary Ombudsman (see p. 40) are required to:

—give facts and analysis with major policy decisions;

—open up internal guidelines about departments' dealings with the public;

—give reasons for administrative decisions to those affected;

—provide information about public services, what they cost, targets, performance, complaints and redress; and

—provide information in response to specific requests on policies, actions and decisions.

As examples of information which departments and public bodies volunteered to the public in 1995, the Ministry of Agriculture, Fisheries and Food made 124 internal guidance documents available through the Helpline Desk in its main library;

[11]For further information see *Government and the Individual: The Citizen's Means of Redress* (Aspects of Britain: HMSO, 1996).

and reports by the Social Services Inspectorate of inspections of Voluntary Children's Homes were made public for the first time.

The Code allows independent review when applicants feel that the Code has not been properly applied. Complainants may be referred to the Parliamentary Ombudsman through an MP. Reports are made to Parliament by the Ombudsman if information has been improperly withheld. A similar Code of Practice on Openness in the NHS came into force in June 1995.

As part of the same openness, the Government is also to propose legislation to provide rights of access to health and safety information and personal records. These rights would add to a number of existing rights of access to information in specific areas such as environmental information.

Committee on Standards in Public Life

The Committee on Standards in Public Life (the Nolan Committee), set up in 1994, issued its first report in May 1995. It recommended, among other things, an independent element in the scrutiny of the conduct of MPs; in the acceptance of appointments by Ministers when they leave office; and of how Ministers make appointments to public bodies. The report also recommended a revision of the rules of behaviour for Ministers (to be known in future as 'Conduct and Procedure for Ministers'). The Government accepted the broad thrust of its recommendations. As a result:

—the first independent Commissioner for Public Appointments was appointed in November 1995. The Commissioner provides advice and guidance to departments and monitors, regulates and audits their procedures for making appointments to executive non-departmental public bodies and NHS bodies, ensuring that appointments are governed by the overriding principle of appointment on merit. The Commissioner published a code of practice in April 1996, and will publish an annual report which sets out the results of the monitoring of all departments' appointments procedures;

—in March 1996 the Government published the proposed text of the revised rules on the acceptance of appointments outside government by former civil servants; this brings special advisers within the system and enables the Prime Minister's Advisory Committee on Business Appointments to announce the reasons for its decisions and to advise a civil servant or Minister that the acceptance of a particular appointment is inappropriate;

—in March 1996 the Government also published a consultation paper which proposes action to improve the accountability of public bodies. *Spending Public Money: Governance and Audit Issues* (see Further Reading) includes a clear set of principles for the audit of public money, including how well it is spent. It also provides a framework for accountability.

(See p. 27 for details of Parliament's acceptance of the Nolan Committee's recommendations on MPs.)

The Civil Service

The Civil Service is concerned with the conduct of the whole range of government activities as they affect the community. These range from policy formulation to carrying out the day-to-day duties of public administration.

Civil servants are servants of the Crown. For all practical purposes the Crown in this context means, and is represented by, the Government of the day. In most circumstances the executive powers of the Crown are exercised by, and on the advice of, Her Majesty's Ministers, who are in turn answerable to Parliament. The Civil Service as such has no constitutional personality or responsibility separate from that of the Government of the day. The duty of the individual civil servant is first and foremost to the Minister of the Crown who is in charge of the department in which he or she is serving. A change of Minister, for whatever reason, does not involve a change of staff. Ministers sometimes appoint special advisers from outside the Civil Service. The advisers are normally paid from public funds, but their appointments come to an end when the Government's term of office finishes, or when the Minister concerned leaves the Government or moves to another appointment.

A new Civil Service code came into force in January 1996, following publication in July 1994 of *The Civil Service: Continuity and Change*, a White Paper on the role and future of the Civil Service. The Code provides a statement of the constitutional framework within which all civil servants work and the values they are expected to uphold. The Code includes an independent line of appeal to the Civil Service Commissioners (see p. 65) on alleged breaches of the Code.

The number of civil servants fell from 732,000 in April 1979 to 499,900 in January 1996, its lowest since 1939. This reflects the Government's policy of controlling the cost of the Civil Service and of improving its efficiency.

About half of all civil servants are engaged in the provision of public services. These include paying sickness benefits and pensions, collecting taxes and contributions, running employment services, staffing prisons, and providing services to industry and agriculture. A quarter are employed in the Ministry of Defence. The rest are divided between central administrative and policy duties; support services; and largely financially self-supporting services, for instance, those provided by the Department for National Savings and the Royal Mint. Four-fifths of civil servants work outside London.

The total also includes members of the Senior Civil Service, around 3,000 of the most senior managers and policy advisers. They are responsible for sustaining core civil service values and for serving the collective interest of government with a focus and loyalty wider than their own departments and agencies.

Equality of Opportunity

The Government is committed to achieving equality of opportunity for all its staff. In support of this commitment, the Civil Service, which recruits and promotes on the basis of merit, is actively pursuing policies to develop career opportunities for women, ethnic minorities and people with disabilities. In April 1995:

—women represented 51.3 per cent of all non-industrial civil servants, and since 1987 the proportion of women in the top three grades of the service has more than doubled to almost 9 per cent;

—representation of ethnic minority staff among non-industrial civil servants had increased from 4.2 per cent in 1989 to 5.5 per cent and compares well with 4.9 per cent, which is the ethnic minority representation in the working population;

—2.8 per cent of disabled people were employed in the non-industrial home Civil Service, of whom 1.6 per cent were registered disabled—just above the proportion of registered disabled people in the workforce as a whole and twice the proportion employed in the private sector.

Progress is monitored and reported on regularly by the Cabinet Office (OPS).

Management Reforms

Civil Service reforms are being implemented to ensure improved management performance, in particular through the increased accountability of individual managers, based on clear objectives and responsibilities. These reforms include performance-related pay schemes and other incentives.

Executive Agencies: Next Steps Programme

The Next Steps Programme, launched in 1988, aims to deliver government services more efficiently and effectively within available resources for the benefit of taxpayers, customers and staff. This has involved setting up, as far as is practicable, separate units or agencies to perform the executive functions of government. Agencies remain part of the Civil Service but under the terms of individual framework documents they enjoy greater delegation of financial, pay and personnel matters. Agencies are headed by chief executives who are accountable to Ministers but who are personally responsible for the day-to-day operations of the agency.

No agency can be established until the 'prior options' of abolition, privatisation and contracting out have been considered and ruled out. These 'prior options' are reconsidered when agencies are reviewed, normally after five years of operation, although Ministers may wish to bring the timescale forward.

At the end of 1995, 109 agencies were in existence, together with 23 Executive Units of Customs and Excise and 27 Executive Offices of the Inland Revenue. At that time 366,000 civil servants—67 per cent of the total—worked in organisations run on Next Steps lines. At the same time a further 57 agency candidates—employing nearly 58,000 staff—had been identified as suitable for agency status.

In 1994–95 overall, agencies met 83 per cent of their key performance targets—a small improvement on the previous year because, in general, targets are made progressively tougher.

Efficiency Measures

In 1992 the Government increased its drive to secure the best value for money in the provision of public services through expanding competition and encouraging private sector involvement. Up to 1992, £20–25 million worth of activities had been opened up to external competition. By March 1995 over £2,600 million of activities, covering 69,000 posts, had been reviewed; and in 1995–96 alone over £1,000 million of activities have been reviewed.

Central Management and Structure

Responsibility for central co-ordination and management of the Civil Service is divided between the Cabinet Office (OPS) and the Treasury.

The OPS, which is under the control of the Prime Minister, as Minister for the Civil Service, oversees organisation, senior civil service pay, pensions and allowances, recruitment, retirement and redundancy policy, personnel management and statistics, and overall efficiency of the Service.

Following the fundamental expenditure review of the Treasury's running costs during 1994,[12] that department's responsibilities for the effective and efficient management of the public sector have been narrowed down to the basic objective of maintaining a financial control system which delivers continuing improvements in the efficiency of government.

The function of official Head of the Home Civil Service is combined with that of Secretary to the Cabinet.

At the senior levels, where management forms a major part of most jobs, there are common grades throughout the Civil Service. These unified grades 1 to 7 are known as the Open Structure and cover grades from Permanent Secretary level to Principal level. Within the unified grades each post is filled by the person best qualified, regardless of the occupational group to which he or she previously belonged.

Below this the structure of the non-industrial Civil Service is based on a system of occupational groups. These groups assist the recruitment and matching of skills to posts and offer career paths in which specialist skills can be developed. Departments and agencies are being encouraged to develop their own pay and grading arrangements. They are expected to produce value-for-money benefits which are greater than those available through centrally controlled negotiation. Since April 1996 all departments and agencies have been responsible for implementing their own systems of pay and grading of staff below senior levels.

[12]In 1993 the Government announced that it would conduct in-depth reviews of all public expenditure by each government department. These reviews examine long-term trends in expenditure, the ways in which services could be delivered more economically and effectively, and areas from which the State could withdraw.

The Diplomatic Service

The Diplomatic Service, a separate service of some 6,000 people, provides the staff for the Foreign & Commonwealth Office (see p. 122) and for British diplomatic missions abroad.

The Diplomatic Service has its own grade structure, linked to that of the Home Civil Service. Terms and conditions of service are comparable, but take into account the special demands of the Service, particularly the requirement to serve abroad. Home civil servants, members of the armed forces and individuals from the private sector may also serve in the Foreign & Commonwealth Office and at overseas posts on loan or attachment.

Civil Service Recruitment

Recruitment is based on the principle of selection on merit by fair and open competition. Independent Civil Service Commissioners are responsible for approving the selection of people for appointment to the Senior Civil Service. Recruitment of all other staff is the responsibility of departments and executive agencies. Departments and agencies can choose whether to undertake this recruitment work themselves, to employ a private sector recruitment agency or to use the Recruitment and Assessment Services Agency to recruit on their behalf.

People from outside the Civil Service may be recruited directly to all levels, particularly to posts requiring skills and experience more readily found in the private sector. The exchange of staff between the Civil Service and industry is also encouraged.

Since May 1995 departments and agencies have been required to publish information about their recruitment systems.

Training

Individual government departments and agencies are responsible for the performance of their own staff. They provide training and development to meet their business needs, to improve performance, and to help staff respond effectively to changing demands. Most training and development takes place within departments and agencies. In addition, the Civil Service College provides management and professional training, mainly for those who occupy, or hope to occupy, relatively senior positions. Considerable use is made of other providers in the private and public sectors.

Civil servants aged under 18 may continue their general education by attending courses, usually for one day a week ('day release' schemes). All staff may be entitled to financial support to continue their education, mainly in their own time. There are also opportunities for civil servants to undertake research and study in areas of interest to them and to their department or agency.

Promotion

Departments are responsible for the deployment of their staff and their progression to higher levels of responsibility. In some cases, centrally arranged postings are supplemented or replaced by job advertising. For about 150 of the most senior posts in the Civil Service, appointments and transfers are approved by the Prime Minister, who is advised by the Head of the Home Civil Service.

Political and Private Activities

Civil servants are required to perform loyally the duties assigned to them by the Government of the day, whatever its political persuasion. It is essential that Ministers and the public should have confidence that the personal views of civil servants do not influence the performance of their official duties, given the role of the Civil Service in serving successive governments formed by different parties. The aim of the rules which govern political activities by civil servants is to allow them, subject to these fundamental principles, the greatest possible freedom to participate in public affairs consistent with their rights and duties as citizens. The rules are therefore concerned with activities liable to give public expression to political views rather than with privately held beliefs and opinions.

The Civil Service is divided into three groups for the purposes of deciding the extent to which individuals may take part in political activities:

—those in the 'politically free' group, consisting of industrial staff and non-office grades, are free to engage in any political activity outside official time, including adoption as a prospective candidate for the British or the European Parliament (although they would have to resign from the Service before giving their consent to nomination);

—those in the 'politically restricted' group, which comprises staff in Grade 7 and above as well as Administration Trainees and Higher Executive Officers (D [development]), may not take part in national political activities but may apply for permission to take part in local political activities; and

—the 'intermediate' group, which comprises all other civil servants, may apply for permission to take part in national or local political activity, apart from candidature for the British or the European Parliament.

Where required, permission is granted to the maximum extent consistent with the Civil Service's reputation for political impartiality and the avoidance of any conflict with official duties. A code of discretion requires moderation and the avoidance of embarrassment to Ministers.

Generally, there are no restrictions on the private activities of civil servants, provided that these do not bring discredit on the Civil Service, and that there is no possibility of conflict with official duties. For instance, a civil servant must comply with any departmental instruction on the need to seek authority before taking part in any outside activity which involves official experience.

Security

Each department is responsible for its own internal security. As a general rule the privately-held political views of civil servants are not a matter of official concern. However, no one may be employed on work which is vital to the security of the State who is, or has been involved in, or associated with, activities threatening national security. Certain posts are not open to people who fall into this category, or to anyone whose reliability may be in doubt for any other reason.

The Security Commission may investigate breaches of security in the public service and advise on changes in security procedure if requested to do so by the Prime Minister after consultation with the Leader of the Opposition.

Local Government

Although Britain's system of local government has its origins in structures developed in Saxon England (see p. 2), the first comprehensive system of local councils was established in the late 19th century. Over the years the range of services for which local authorities are responsible has grown and this has been one of the factors which has led to reforms in the pattern of local government.

Local Government Reform

A major reform of local government took place in 1974 in England and Wales and in 1975 in Scotland. This created two main tiers of local authority throughout England and Wales: counties and the smaller districts. Local government in London had been reorganised along the same lines in 1965. In Scotland, functions were allocated to regions and districts on the mainland; single-tier authorities were introduced for the three Islands areas. In Northern Ireland changes were made in 1973 which replaced the two-tier county council and urban/rural council system with a single-tier district council system.

The Local Government Act 1985 abolished the Greater London Council and the six metropolitan county councils in England. Most of their functions were transferred to the London boroughs and metropolitan district councils respectively in 1986 (see p. 72).

Local Government Commission

The Local Government Act 1992 made provision for the establishment of a Local Government Commission to review the structure, boundaries and electoral arrangements of local government in England. The Commission, set up in 1992, has reviewed the structure of local government in non-metropolitan England. The reviews considered whether the two-tier structure should be replaced by single-tier ('unitary') authorities in each area; for the most part the Commission recommended the retention of two-tier government, but suggested unitary authorities for some areas, especially the larger cities. The first changes, on the Isle of Wight, were implemented in April 1995. Thirteen more unitary authorities followed in April 1996, and others will be set up from April 1997. The Commission is now concentrating on reviews of local authority electoral arrangements, although it may also look at the boundaries of metropolitan areas where there is sufficient demand.

Scotland and Wales

Legislation to affect changes in Scotland and Wales[13] took effect from April 1996. On mainland Scotland, 29 new single-tier councils have replaced the previous system of regional and district councils. The three Islands' councils remain. In Wales, 22 new single-tier councils have replaced the previous system of county councils and district councils. The first elections for the new councils took place in April 1995 for Scotland and May 1995 for Wales, with the new authorities acting in 'shadow' form until April 1996 to make preparations for their assumption of power.

[13] The Local Government etc. (Scotland) Act 1994 and the Local Government (Wales) Act 1994.

Local Authorities' Powers

Local authorities derive their power from legislation. Although local authorities are responsible for administering certain services, Ministers have powers in some areas to secure a degree of uniformity in standards to safeguard public health or to protect the rights of individual citizens.

Relations with Central Government

The main link between local authorities and central government in England is the Department of the Environment. However, other departments such as the Department for Education and Employment and the Home Office are also concerned with various local government functions. In the rest of Britain the local authorities deal with the Scottish or Welsh Offices or the Department of the Environment for Northern Ireland, as appropriate.

Principal Types of Local Authority

Before the recent reforms, England outside Greater London was divided into counties, sub-divided into districts. All the districts and the non-metropolitan counties had locally elected councils with separate functions. County councils provided large-scale services such as education and social services, while district councils were responsible for the more local ones (see p. 75). These arrangements will broadly continue in areas where two-tier local government will remain. The new unitary authorities, where they are being created, bring all of these local authority functions together.

Greater London is divided into 32 boroughs and the City of London, each of which has a council responsible for local government in its area. In the six metropolitan counties there are 36 district councils; there are no county councils. A number of services, however, require a statutory authority over areas wider than the individual boroughs and districts. These are:

—waste disposal (in certain areas);

—the fire services, including civil defence; and

—(outside London) public transport.

These are run by joint authorities composed of elected councillors nominated by the borough or district councils. Local councils also provide many of the members of the police authorities.

In addition to the two-tier local authority system in England, over 8,000 parish councils or meetings provide and manage local facilities such as allotments and village halls and act as agents for other district council functions. They also provide a forum for discussion of local issues. In Wales around 730 community councils have similar functions, and provision is made for local community councils in Scotland.

The boundaries and electoral arrangements of local authorities in Wales and Scotland are kept under review by the Local Government Boundary Commissions for Wales and Scotland respectively. In 1992 the responsibilities of the former Local Government Boundary Commission for England passed to the Local Government Commission (see p. 70).

In Northern Ireland, 26 district councils are responsible for local environmental and certain other services. Statutory bodies, such as the Northern Ireland Housing Executive and area boards, are responsible to central government departments for administering other major services (see p. 76).

Election of Councils

Local councils consist of elected councillors. Councillors are paid a basic allowance but may also be entitled to additional allowances and expenses for attending meetings or taking on special responsibilities. Parish and community councillors cannot claim allowances for duties undertaken within their own council areas. In Scotland community councillors are not eligible for any form of allowance.

In England and Wales each council elects its presiding officer annually. Some districts have the ceremonial title of borough, or city, both granted by royal authority. In boroughs and cities the presiding officer is normally known as the Mayor. In the City of London and certain other large cities, he or she is known as the Lord Mayor. In Scotland the presiding officer of the council of each of the four cities is called the Lord Provost. In other councils he or she is known as a convenor or provost. In Northern Ireland district councils are presided over by a chairman; there are a number of boroughs and cities where the presiding officer is the Mayor and in Belfast he or she is known as the Lord Mayor. In Wales the presiding officer of the new authorities is called chairman in the case of counties and mayor in the case of county boroughs.

Councillors are elected for four years. All county councils in England, London borough councils, and about two-thirds of non-metropolitan district councils are elected in their entirety every four years. In the remaining districts (including all metropolitan districts) one-third of the councillors are elected in each of the three years when county council elections are not held. Where new unitary authorities are to be set up in England, Parliamentary Orders make the necessary provisions regarding elections. In Scotland the next elections of whole councils will be held in 1999, with others due at three-year intervals after that. In Wales elections of whole councils will continue to be held every four years, again with the next due in 1999.

Voters

Anyone may vote at a local government election in Britain provided he or she is:

—aged 18 years or over;

—a citizen of Britain or of another Commonwealth country, or of the Irish Republic, or (since 1996) a citizen of the European Union;

—not legally disqualified; and

—on the electoral register.

To qualify for registration a person must be resident in the council area on the qualifying date. In Northern Ireland there are slightly different requirements.

Candidates

Most candidates at local government elections stand as representatives of a national political party, although some stand as independents. Candidates must be British citizens, other Commonwealth citizens or citizens of the European Union, and aged 21 or over. In addition, they must either:

—be registered as local electors in the area of the relevant local authority; or

—have occupied (as owner or tenant) land or premises in that area during the whole of the preceding 12 months; or

—have had their main place of work in the area throughout this 12-month period.

No-one may be elected to a council of which he or she is an employee, and there are some other disqualifications. All candidates for district council elections in Northern Ireland are required to make a declaration against terrorism.

Electoral Divisions and Procedure

Counties in England are divided into electoral divisions, each returning one councillor. Districts in England and Northern Ireland are divided into wards, returning one councillor or more. In Scotland the electoral areas in the new councils are called wards and in Wales they are called electoral divisions; each returns one or more councillors. Parishes (in England) and communities (in Wales) may be divided into wards. Wards return at least one councillor. The minimum parish/community council size is five councillors.

The procedure for local government voting in Great Britain is broadly similar to that for parliamentary elections. In Northern Ireland local government elections are held by proportional representation, and electoral wards are grouped into district electoral areas.

Council Functions and Services

At present in England county councils are responsible for strategic planning, transport planning, highways, traffic regulation, education,[14] consumer protection, refuse disposal, police,[15]

---

[14]Schools may, however, 'opt out' of local education authority control by obtaining grant-maintained status. For further information, see *Education* (Aspects of Britain: HMSO, 1996).

[15]In many areas, police forces cover more than one county, and in these cases a joint board is set up to act as police authority.

the fire service, libraries and the personal social services. District councils are responsible for services such as environmental health, housing, decisions on most local planning applications, and refuse collection. Both tiers of local authority have powers to provide facilities such as museums, art galleries and parks; arrangements depend on local agreement. Where unitary authorities are created in non-metropolitan areas, they will be responsible for both county and district level functions.

In the metropolitan counties the district councils are responsible for all services apart from the police, the fire service and public transport and, in some areas, waste regulation and disposal (see p. 72). In Greater London the boroughs and the Corporation of the City of London have similar functions, but London's metropolitan police force is responsible to the Home Secretary. Responsibility for public transport lies with London Transport.

In mainland Scotland, as in Wales, new single-tier councils came into effect in April 1996, taking over all local government functions.

In Northern Ireland local environmental and certain other services, such as leisure and the arts, are administered by the district councils. Responsibility for planning, roads, water supply and sewerage services is exercised in each district through a divisional office of the Department of the Environment for Northern Ireland. Area boards, responsible to central departments, administer education, public libraries and the health and personal social services locally. The Northern Ireland Housing Executive, responsible to the Department of the Environment for Northern Ireland, administers housing.

The Government introduced legislation in 1980 and 1988 which aimed to encourage local authorities to obtain value for money in the services they provide. As a result many local government services which were traditionally provided in-house, such as refuse collection and leisure management, must now be submitted to competition from private firms ('compulsory competitive tendering'—CCT). In-house teams may also bid for the work. The Government estimates that CCT has resulted in a cost saving of 7 per cent since its introduction It has now been extended to local authorities' provision of a range of professional services, such as legal and personnel services. The metropolitan districts and London boroughs have already introduced some of these new arrangements and they will be extended to the remaining authorities over the next few years.

Changes in Local Government

There have been numerous changes in recent years in the way that local authorities approach their responsibilities. Many of these can be encapsulated under the term 'the enabling authority'. This is used to describe the general shift away from local authorities providing services directly and towards their arranging for services to be provided, or carrying out functions in partnership with other bodies. For example, councils often have nomination rights to housing association properties, so that they are acting not as provider but as 'gatekeeper'. Likewise, under the community care reforms, councils with social services responsibilities draw up care plans for those who need them, but the care is often provided by the private or voluntary sectors funded by the council, rather than directly by the local authority itself.

Internal Organisation of Local Authorities

Local authorities have considerable freedom to make arrangements for carrying out their duties; these are set out in standing orders. Some decisions are made by the full council; many other matters are delegated to committees composed of members of the council. A council may delegate most functions to a committee or officer, although certain powers are legally reserved to the council as a whole. The powers and duties of local authority committees are usually laid down in the terms of reference. Parish and community councils in England and Wales are often able to do their work in full session, although they appoint committees from time to time as necessary.

In England and Wales committees generally have to reflect the political composition of the council (although the legislation governing this specifically excludes parish or community councils). In practice, this is often also the case in Scotland, although it is not enforced by legislation. People who are not members of the council may be co-opted onto decision-making committees and can speak and take part in debates; they cannot normally vote. Legislation also prevents senior officers and others in politically sensitive posts from being members of another local authority or undertaking public political activity. Some of these provisions have not been introduced in Northern Ireland.

The Government is looking at ways of improving the internal management of local authorities.

Public Access

The public (including the press) are admitted to council, committee and sub-committee meetings, and have access to agendas, reports and minutes of meetings and certain background papers.

Local authorities may exclude the public from meetings and withhold these papers only in limited circumstances.

Employees

About 1.4 million people[16] are employed by local authorities in England. These include administrative, professional and technical staff, teachers, firefighters, and manual workers. Education is the largest service, employing some 40 per cent of all local government workers. Councils are individually responsible, within certain national legislative requirements, for deciding the structure of their workforces.

Senior staff appointments are usually made by the elected councillors. More junior appointments are made by heads of departments. Pay and conditions of service are usually a matter for each council, although there are scales recommended by national negotiating machinery between authorities and trade unions, and most authorities follow these.

Local Authority Finance

Local government expenditure accounts for about 25 per cent of public spending. The Government has sought to influence local government spending as part of a general policy of controlling the growth of public expenditure. Since 1984 the Government has had powers to limit or 'cap' local authority budgets (local authority taxation in Scotland) by setting a maximum amount for local authorities which have, in its view, set budgets which are excessive.

In 1995–96 expenditure by local authorities in Britain was about £74,800 million. Current expenditure amounted to £64,000

[16]Full-time equivalents.

million, and capital expenditure, net of capital receipts, was £6,700 million and debt interest £4,100 million. Local government capital expenditure is financed primarily by borrowing within limits set by central government and from capital receipts from the disposal of land and buildings.

System of Finance
Local authorities in Great Britain (but not Northern Ireland) raise revenue from three main sources:

—central government grants;

—non-domestic rates; and

—the council tax.

Non-domestic rates are a tax on the occupiers of non-domestic property. The rateable value of property is assessed by reference to annual rents and reviewed every five years. In England and Wales the non-domestic rate is set nationally by central government and collected by local authorities. It is paid into a national pool and redistributed to local authorities in proportion to their population. In Scotland non-domestic rates are levied by local authorities. In Northern Ireland rates are not payable on industrial premises or on commercial premises in enterprise zones.

Domestic property is subject to the council tax. Each dwelling is allocated to one of eight valuation bands, depending on its estimated open market value in April 1991. Tax levels are set by local authorities, but the relationship between the tax for each band is fixed. Discounts are available for dwellings with fewer than two resident adults. People on low incomes are entitled to rebates of up to 100 per cent on their tax bill.

In Northern Ireland district councils continue to raise revenue through the levying of domestic rates; these are collected by local authorities.

Control of Finance
Local councils normally have a finance committee to keep their financial policy under constant review. Their annual accounts must be audited by independent auditors appointed by the Audit Commission in England and Wales, or by the Commission for Local Authority Accounts in Scotland. In Northern Ireland this role is exercised by the chief local government auditor who is appointed by the Department of the Environment for Northern Ireland.

Local Government Complaints System
Local authorities are encouraged to resolve complaints through internal mechanisms, and members of the public will often ask their own councillor for assistance in this. Local authorities must also appoint a monitoring officer, whose duties include ensuring that the local authority acts lawfully in the conduct of its business.

Allegations of local government maladministration may be investigated by statutory independent Commissioners for Local Administration, often known as 'local government ombudsmen'. There are three of these in England, and one each in Wales and Scotland. A report is issued on each complaint fully investigated and, if injustice caused by maladministration is found, the local ombudsman normally proposes a remedy. The council must consider the report and reply to it.

An independent review of the local government ombudsman service in England began in July 1995.

In Northern Ireland a Commissioner for Complaints deals with complaints alleging injustices suffered as a result of maladministration by district councils and certain other public bodies.

Administration of Welsh, Scottish and Northern Ireland Affairs

Wales

Following the Roman withdrawal from Britain in the fifth century and the invasions by the Angles, Saxons and Jutes from northern Europe, the Britons maintained an independent existence in Wales. The country remained a Celtic stronghold, but was subject to English influence. In the late 13th century Edward I of England launched a successful campaign to bring Wales under English rule. Wales was placed for the most part under the same laws as England and in 1301 Edward's eldest son—later Edward II—was created Prince of Wales, a title which is still normally given to the eldest son of the Sovereign. Following the accession to the English throne in 1485 of Henry VII of the Welsh House of Tudor, the Acts of Union of 1536 and 1542 united England and Wales administratively, politically and legally.

Today substantial administrative autonomy for Wales is centred on the Secretary of State for Wales, who is a member of the Cabinet and has wide-ranging responsibilities for the economy, education, welfare services and the provision of amenities. These are exercised through the Welsh Office (see p. 84). Wales is represented at Westminster by 38 Members of Parliament; special arrangements exist for the discussion of Welsh affairs (see p. 34).

Local government in Wales, which is exercised through a system of elected authorities similar to that in England, has been reorganised. In April 1996, 22 new single-tier councils replaced the former 8 county councils and 37 district councils (see p. 70). The legal system in Wales is identical with the English one (see p. 102).

Welsh Office
Cathays Park, Cardiff CF1 3NQ. Tel: 01222 825111
Gwydyr House, Whitehall, London SW1A 2ER. Tel: 0171 270 3000

Responsibilities
The Welsh Office is responsible for many aspects of Welsh affairs, including: health, community care and personal social services; education, except for terms and conditions of service, student awards and the University of Wales; Welsh language and culture; agriculture and fisheries; forestry; local government; housing; water and sewerage; environmental protection; sport; land use, including town and country planning; countryside and nature conservation; new towns; ancient monuments and historic buildings; arts, museums and libraries.

The Department's responsibilities also include: roads; tourism; enterprise and training; selective financial assistance to industry; the Urban Programme and urban investment grants in Wales; the operation of the European Regional Development Fund in Wales and other European Union matters; women's issues; non-departmental public bodies; civil emergencies; all financial aspects of these matters, including Welsh revenue support grant; and oversight responsibilities for economic affairs and regional planning in Wales.

Executive Agency
CADW: Welsh Historic Monuments

Scotland

A united kingdom first emerged in Scotland in the ninth century. Throughout the Middle Ages there was intermittent warfare between Scotland and England. When the childless Elizabeth I of England died in 1603, James VI of Scotland was her nearest heir. He became, in addition, James I of England; and England, Wales and Scotland collectively became known as Great Britain. However, apart from the union of the crowns, England and Scotland remained separate political entities during the 17th century, except for a period of enforced unification under Oliver Cromwell in the 1650s (see p. 3). In 1707 both countries were joined together under the Act of Union, which created a single parliament for Great Britain. Scotland retained its own system of law and church settlement.

Today Scotland continues to have its own legal (see p. 106) and church systems; it also has wide administrative autonomy. Separate Acts of Parliament are passed for Scotland where appropriate, and there are special arrangements for considering Scottish business in Parliament (see p. 34). The distinctive conditions and needs of Scotland and its people are reflected in separate Scottish legislation on many domestic matters. Special provisions applying to Scotland alone are also inserted in Acts which otherwise apply to Britain generally. Scotland is represented at Westminster by 72 Members of Parliament.

The Secretary of State for Scotland, a Cabinet minister, has responsibility in Scotland for a wide range of economic and social functions (see p. 86). These are exercised through The

Scottish Office, which has its headquarters in Edinburgh and an office in London.

Review of Scottish Government
In 1993 the Government issued a White Paper, *Scotland and the Union: A Partnership for Good,* following a wide-ranging examination of Scotland's place in Britain and the role of Parliament in Scottish affairs. Certain functions have been transferred from Whitehall departments to The Scottish Office. For example, responsibility for training policy in Scotland and the Scottish Arts Council was transferred to The Scottish Office in April 1994. In order to increase the responsiveness of The Scottish Office to the people of Scotland, a central enquiry unit and information points are being established in many towns.

Local government in Scotland, which generally operates on a two-tier basis broadly similar to that in England and Wales, has been reorganised. In April 1996 29 new single-tier councils replaced the former 62 regional and district councils.

The Scottish Office
St Andrew's House, Edinburgh EH1 3DG. Tel: 0131 556 8400
Dover House, Whitehall, London SW1A 2AU. Tel: 0171 270 3000

Responsibilities
The Scottish Office is responsible for a wide range of policy matters. These include: agriculture and fisheries; education; law and order; environmental protection and conservation of the countryside; land-use planning; local government; housing; roads and certain aspects of transport services; social work and health.

The Secretary of State for Scotland also has a major role

in planning and development of the Scottish economy, and important functions relating to industrial development, including responsibility for financial assistance to industry.

The Secretary of State for Scotland has overall responsibility for legal services in Scotland and is advised by the two Scottish Law Officers—the Lord Advocate and the Solicitor General for Scotland (see p. 89).

The Scottish Office's responsibilities are discharged principally through its five departments. There are also three smaller departments: the Registers of Scotland and the Scottish Record Office (which are executive agencies) and the General Register Office for Scotland.

Relations with Other Government Departments

Other government departments with significant Scottish responsibilities have offices in Scotland and work closely with The Scottish Office.

Scottish Departments

An outline of the functions of the main Scottish departments is given below.

Scottish Office Agriculture, Environment and Fisheries Department

Promotion and regulation of agriculture: safeguarding public, food, plant and animal health and welfare; land use and forestry, livestock subsidies and commodities. Environment, including environmental protection, nature conservation and the countryside; water supplies and sewerage services; sustainable development. Promotion and regulation of fisheries; protection of the marine environment;

research on and monitoring of fish stocks; enforcement of fisheries laws and regulations.

Executive Agencies
Scottish Agricultural Science Agency.
Scottish Fisheries Protection Agency.

Scottish Office Development Department
Housing and area regeneration; new towns; local government organisation and finance; transport and local roads, Roads Directorate; co-ordination of Scottish Office European interests; land-use planning; building control; protection and presentation to the public of historic buildings and ancient monuments.

Executive Agency
Historic Scotland.

Scottish Office Education and Industry Department
Industrial and regional economic development matters; exports, technology; Highlands and Islands co-ordination; enterprise and tourism; industrial expansion; energy; training; education; student awards; arts (including the National Institutions), libraries, museums and galleries, Gaelic language; sport and recreation.

Executive Agencies
The Scottish Office Pensions Agency.
Student Award Agency for Scotland.

Scottish Office Department of Health
National Health Service; Chief Scientist's Office; Public Health Policy Unit.

Scottish Office Home Department and Scottish Courts Administration

Central administration of law and order (includes police service, criminal justice and licensing, legal aid, the Scottish Court Service and the Scottish Prison Service), civil law, fire, home defence and civil emergency services; social work services; Solicitor's Office.

Executive Agencies
Scottish Court Service.
Scottish Prison Service.

Central services are provided to the five Scottish departments. These include the office of the Solicitor to the Secretary of State, The Scottish Office Information Directorate, the Directorate of Administrative Services, Finance and the Personnel Group.

The following departments are directly responsible to the Law Officers and are not part of The Scottish Office:

Lord Advocate's Department

2 Carlton Gardens, London SW1Y 5AA. Tel: 0171 210 1010
Provision of legal advice to the Government on issues affecting Scotland; responsibility for drafting government primary legislation relating to Scotland and adapting for Scotland other primary legislation. Provision of advice in matters of parliamentary procedures affecting Scotland.

Crown Office

25 Chambers Street, Edinburgh EH1 1LA. Tel: 0131 226 2626
Control of all prosecutions in Scotland.

Northern Ireland

During the tenth century Ireland was dominated by the Vikings[17]. In the 12th century Henry II of England launched an invasion of Ireland. Although a large part of the country came under the control of Anglo-Norman magnates, England exercised little direct control of Ireland during the Middle Ages. The Tudor monarchs showed a much greater tendency to intervene in Ireland and in 1541 Henry VIII assumed the title of King of Ireland. During the reign of Elizabeth I a series of campaigns was waged against Irish insurgents. The main focus of resistance was the province of Ulster. After the collapse of this resistance in 1607, Ulster was settled by large numbers of English and Scottish Protestants, their religion setting them apart from the indigenous Roman Catholic inhabitants of Ireland.

Northern Ireland consists of six of the nine counties of the former province of Ulster. These remained part of Britain when, in 1922, the 26 counties of Southern Ireland became the Irish Free State, a self-governing state outside Britain. In 1949 the Irish Free State became the Irish Republic, a fully independent republic outside the Commonwealth.

Between 1921 and 1972 Northern Ireland had its own Parliament and Government, subordinate to the Parliament at Westminster. The domination of the Parliament by the Protestant majority population, descendants of the Scottish and English settlers, led to resentment among the Roman Catholic community. This was an important factor behind the active broad-based civil rights movement which emerged in 1967, with the aim of winning social and economic reforms in order to place Roman Catholics on an equal footing with Protestants. Some Protestants

[17]For more information see *Northern Ireland* (Aspects of Britain: HMSO,1995).

regarded the movement as a threat and street demonstrations were increasingly marked by sectarian disturbances. In 1969 the Northern Ireland Government asked Westminster to provide additional army troops to support the severely over-extended police force. Subsequently sectarian divisions were exploited by terrorists from both sides, the nature of the violence changing fundamentally from a public order problem to a terrorist one.

The Northern Ireland Government had responsibility for local affairs but not for defence and the armed forces, foreign and trade policies, and taxation and customs. In 1972, with violence continuing, the British Government decided to take on responsibility for law and order. This was unacceptable to the Northern Ireland Government, which resigned in protest, the result being the introduction of direct rule from Westminster in 1972.

Over the past 25 years British governments have attempted to find the basis for returning greater power to Northern Ireland's locally elected representatives but agreement has proved elusive. The Anglo-Irish Agreement in 1985 gave new impetus to co-operation between Britain and Ireland on matters affecting Northern Ireland. From 1990 the Government has sought a widely acceptable and comprehensive political settlement encompassing all the relevant relationships: those within Northern Ireland itself, those within the island of Ireland, and those between the British and Irish Governments, through the promotion of round-table talks in 1991 and 1992 and by bilateral discussions with the main Northern Ireland constitutional parties—the Ulster Unionists, Democratic Unionists, the Social Democratic and Labour Party and the Alliance Party—and also with the Irish Government.

In December 1993, the Prime Minister, John Major, and his Irish counterpart, Albert Reynolds, signed a joint declaration setting out a framework of the political realities and constitutional principles which would inform the search for a political settlement. Both Governments pledged that they would seek—together with the Northern Ireland constitutional political parties—to create institutions and structures enabling the people of Ireland to work together in all areas of common interest and to build the trust needed to end past divisions.

Recent Developments

In November 1995 the British and Irish Governments launched a Twin Track Initiative which addressed the issues of decommissioning of illegal arms through the establishment of an International Body and preparatory discussions with the parties on ground rules for political negotiations.

Chaired by former US senator George Mitchell, the International Body published its report in January 1996. It concluded that the paramilitary organisations would not decommission any arms before all-party talks and set out six principles of democracy and non-violence to which it said all parties should adhere. In addition, it set out guidelines on ways of decommissioning and proposed several confidence-building measures including, if it were broadly acceptable, an elective process, appropriately mandated and within the talks structure. All of these proposals were endorsed by the British Government.

The Irish Republican Army (IRA) announced the end of its ceasefire on 9 February 1996, and IRA explosions subsequently occurred in London. On 28 February the British and Irish Prime Ministers set a date for all-party negotiations to begin in June 1996 following an election in Northern Ireland. The two

Governments also agreed that until there was an unequivocal restoration of the IRA ceasefire there could be no question of ministerial meetings with Sinn Fein (the political wing of the IRA) or of Sinn Fein taking part in the negotiations.

Following intensive consultations with the Northern Ireland parties in March, the Government published draft elections legislation together with ground rules for the negotiations, and under an Act which came into force on 29 April 1996, 110 delegates were elected in Northern Ireland on 30 May. Participants in the negotiations, which opened on 10 June, were chosen from the 110 delegates who, under the Act, also constituted a purely deliberative forum to discuss issues relevant to promoting dialogue and understanding. The Act also enables a referendum to be held in Northern Ireland on the outcome of the negotiations which the Government hopes will lead to a comprehensive and widely acceptable settlement in the province.

Administration

Under the system of direct rule, the British Parliament approves all laws, and Northern Ireland's government departments are controlled by the Secretary of State—a Cabinet Minister—and his ministerial team. At present 17 MPs are elected to the House of Commons. (This will change to 18 members after the next general election—see p. 20). There is provision for Northern Ireland MPs to debate business relating to Northern Ireland in Parliament (see p. 34).

Local government is the responsibility of 26 district councils (see p. 72).

Northern Ireland Office
Stormont Castle, Belfast BT4 3ST. Tel: 01232 520700
Whitehall, London SW1A 2AZ. Tel: 0171 210 3000

Responsibilities
The Secretary of State for Northern Ireland is the Cabinet
Minister responsible for Northern Ireland. Through the Northern Ireland Office the Secretary of State is directly responsible
for constitutional matters, law and order, security and electoral
matters.

Executive Agencies
The Compensation Agency
Forensic Science Agency of Northern Ireland
Northern Ireland Prison Service

The work of the Northern Ireland departments, whose functions are listed below, is also subject to the direction and control
of the Secretary of State.

Department of Agriculture for Northern Ireland
Development of agri-food, forestry and fisheries industries; veterinary, scientific and development services; food and farming policy;
agri-environment policy and rural development.

**Department of Economic Development for Northern
Ireland**
Promotion of inward investment and development of larger home
industry through the Industrial Development Board; promotion of
enterprise and small business (through the Local Enterprise Development Unit); training and employment services; promotion of

---

industrially relevant research and development and technology transfer; promotion and development of tourism (through the Northern Ireland Tourist Board); energy; mineral development; company regulation; consumer protection; health and safety at work; industrial relations; and equal opportunity in employment and Northern Ireland-wide co-ordination of deregulation.

Executive Agencies
Industrial Research and Technology Unit
Training and Employment Agency (Northern Ireland)

Department of Education for Northern Ireland
Control of the five education and library boards and education from nursery to further and higher education; youth services; sport and recreation; the arts and culture (including libraries); and the development of community relations within and between schools.

Department of the Environment for Northern Ireland
Most of the Department's functions are carried out by eleven Next Steps agencies. These include: planning, roads, water and construction services; environmental protection and conservation services; land registries, public records, ordnance survey, rate collection, driver and vehicle testing and licensing. Core departmental functions include: overall responsibility for housing and transport policies; fire services; certain controls over local government; disposal and management of the Department's land and property holdings; and urban regeneration.

Executive Agencies
Construction Service

Driver and Vehicle Licensing Northern Ireland
Driver and Vehicle Testing Agency
Environment and Heritage Service
Land Registers Northern Ireland
Ordnance Survey of Northern Ireland
Planning Service
Public Record Office of Northern Ireland
Rate Collection Agency
Roads Service
Water Service

Department of Finance and Personnel
Control of public expenditure; liaison with HM Treasury and the
Northern Ireland Office on financial matters, economic and social
research and analysis; EC co-ordination; policies for equal opportunities and personnel management; central management and control of the Northern Ireland Civil Service.

Executive Agencies
Government Purchasing Agency
Northern Ireland Research and Statistics Agency
Valuation and Lands Agency

**Department of Health and Social Services for Northern
Ireland**
Health and personal social services and social legislation. Responsibility for the administration of all social security benefits and the
collection of National Insurance contributions.

Executive Agencies
Northern Ireland Child Support Agency
Health Estates Agency
Northern Ireland Social Security Agency

Pressure Groups

Pressure groups are informal organisations which aim to influence Parliament and Government in the way decisions are made and carried out, to the benefit of their members and the causes they support. There is a huge range of groups, covering politics, business, employment, consumer affairs, ethnic minorities, aid to developing countries, foreign relations, education, culture, defence, religion, sport, transport, social welfare, animal welfare and the environment. Some have over a million members, others only a few dozen. Some exert pressure on a number of different issues; others are concerned with a single issue. Some have come to play a recognised role in the way Britain is governed; others seek influence through radical protest.

While political parties seek to win political power, pressure groups aim to influence those who are in power, rather than to exercise the responsibility of government and to legislate.

Pressure Groups and Policy

Pressure groups operating at a national level have a number of methods for influencing the way Britain is governed. Action by them may highlight a particular problem, which is then acknowledged by the Government. Groups whose scale of membership indicates that they are broadly representative in their field may then be consulted by a government department, or take part in Whitehall working groups or advisory councils. If the Government considers that legislation is necessary, proposals are drafted and then circulated to interested groups for their comments.

Legislation is then put before Parliament, and at various times during the passage of a Bill—especially at the committee stage—pressure groups have opportunities to influence its content. If the Act includes delegated legislation (see p. 32), pressure groups may be consulted and have the opportunity to provide information and express their views.

Pressure Groups and Government

The principle of consultation to gain the consent and co-operation of as wide a range of organisations as possible, and ensure the smooth working of laws and regulations, plays an important part in the relationship between government departments and interested groups.

In some instances a department is under legal obligation to consult interested groups. The Government has a duty to consult organised interests, providing the pressure groups involved have a broad enough membership for them to represent a majority view, and provided that they observe confidentiality about their discussions with the department. Members of pressure groups have direct expertise, and an awareness of what is practicable, and can give advice and information to civil servants engaged in preparing policy or legislation. In return, the pressure groups have the opportunity to express their opinions directly to the Government. The contacts between civil servants and pressure group representatives may be relatively informal—by letter or telephone—or more formal, through involvement in working parties or by giving evidence to committees of inquiry.

Administration by Pressure Groups
As well as providing information and opinions, pressure groups can also be involved in administering government policy. The

Law Society—the representative body for solicitors—administered the Government's Legal Aid scheme until that function
was taken over in 1989 by the Legal Aid Board. The Government also makes grants to pressure groups which, as well as
speaking on behalf of their members or for an issue, also provide
a service. Relate: National Marriage Guidance has received
grants for the advice centres it runs, and government departments make grants to a number of pressure groups for research
relating to public policy.

Pressure Groups and Parliament

Lobbying—the practice of approaching MPs or Lords, persuad-
ing them to act on behalf of a cause, and enabling them to do
so by providing advice and information—is a form of pressure
group activity which has substantially increased in recent years.

A common pressure group tactic is to ask members of the
public to write to their MP about an issue—for example, the
Sunday trading laws, or the plight of political prisoners in particular countries—in order to raise awareness and persuade the
MP to support the cause.

Raising Issues in Parliament

Other ways through which pressure groups may exert influence
include:

—suggesting to MPs or Lords subjects for Private Members'
Bills (see p. 29); many pressure groups have ready-drafted
legislation waiting to be sponsored;

—approaching MPs or Lords to ask parliamentary questions as
a means of gaining information from the Government and of
drawing public attention to an issue;

—suggesting to MPs subjects for Early Day Motions (see p. 38); and

—orchestrating public petitions as a form of protest against government policy, or to call for action. If the petition is to be presented in Parliament, it must be worded according to Commons or Lords rules, and be presented by an MP or Lord in his or her own House.

Parliamentary Lobbyists

Many pressure groups employ full-time parliamentary workers or liaison officers, whose job is to develop contacts with MPs and Lords sympathetic to their cause, and to brief them when issues affecting the group are raised in Parliament.

There are also public relations and political consultancy firms specialising in lobbying Parliament and Government. Such firms are employed by pressure groups—as well as by British and overseas companies and organisations—to monitor parliamentary business, and to promote their clients' interests where they are affected by legislation and debate.

The Judiciary and the Administration of the Law

Law

Although Britain is a unitary state, England and Wales, Scotland and Northern Ireland all have their own legal systems, with considerable differences in law, organisation and practice. All three have separate prosecution, prison and police services. Crime prevention policy and non-custodial treatment of offenders are similar throughout Britain. There are different civil court and civil law systems in England and Wales and in Scotland; Northern Ireland's system is in many ways similar to the English and Welsh model.

Common Law and Statute Law

One of the main sources of law in England and Wales and in Northern Ireland is common law, which has evolved over centuries from judges' decisions. The origins of the common law lie in the work of the king's judges after the Norman Conquest of 1066. In seeking to bring together into a single body of legal principles the various local customs of the Anglo-Saxons, great reliance was placed on precedent: the reporting of cases, which assisted in establishing precedents, began in the 13th century. Common law, which continues to be deduced from custom and interpreted in court cases by judges, has never been precisely defined or codified. It forms the basis of the law except when superseded by legislation. In Scotland, too, the doctrine of legal precedent has been more strictly applied since the end of the 18th century.

Much of the law, particularly that relating to criminal justice, is statute law passed by Parliament. If a court reaches a decision which is contrary to the intentions of Parliament, then Parliament must either accept the decision or pass amending legislation. Some Acts create new law, while others are passed to draw together existing law on a given topic. Parliament can repeal a statute and replace it with another.

European Community Law

European Community law, which applies to Britain by virtue of its membership of the European Union, derives from the European Community treaties and the legislation adopted under them. EC legislation has been adopted in most of the fields covered by the Community treaties, including economic and social matters, agriculture and the environment. National courts are bound to apply EC law where it is relevant to cases before them, and can refer cases to the European Court of Justice (see p. 111) for a preliminary ruling on the proper interpretation of EC law. Rulings of the European Court of Justice are binding on Community institutions and member states.

Branches of the Law

There are two main branches of the law; criminal and civil.

—Criminal law is concerned with acts punishable by the State.

—Civil law covers:

   —disputes between individuals about their rights, duties and obligations; and

—dealings between individuals and companies, and between one company and another.

The distinction between the two branches of the law is reflected in the procedures used, the courts in which cases may be heard and the sanctions which may be applied.

The Judiciary

The judiciary is independent of the executive; its adjudications are not subject to ministerial direction or control. The highest judicial appointments are made by the Queen on the advice of the Prime Minister.

The Lord Chancellor is head of the judiciary (except in Scotland), is a senior Cabinet Minister and the Speaker of the House of Lords (see p. 17). This is a unique appointment given that the Lord Chancellor is a member of the judiciary, the executive and the legislature. His administrative responsibility for the Supreme Court (comprising the Court of Appeal, High Court and Crown Court) and the county courts in England and Wales is exercised through the Court Service executive agency. He also has ministerial responsibility for the locally administered magistrates' courts in England and Wales . He advises the Crown on the appointment of most members of the higher judiciary, and he appoints district judges, recorders and lay magistrates as well as an array of tribunal members in England and Wales. In addition he is responsible for promoting general reforms of the civil law and for the legal aid schemes. In Scotland the Secretary of State recommends the appointment of all judges other than the most senior ones. Judges are normally appointed from practising barristers, advocates (in Scotland) or solicitors.

The Courts in England and Wales

Criminal Courts
Summary or less serious offences, which make up the vast majority of criminal cases, are tried in England and Wales by unpaid lay magistrates—justices of the peace (JPs), although in areas with a heavy workload there are a number of full-time, stipendiary magistrates; both sit without a jury. More serious offences are tried by the Crown Court, presided over by a judge sitting with a jury. The Crown Court sits at about 90 centres and is presided over by High Court judges, full-time 'Circuit Judges' and part-time recorders.

Appeals from the magistrates' courts go before the Crown Court or the High Court. Appeals from the Crown Court are made to the Court of Appeal (Criminal Division). The House of Lords is the final appeal court in all cases.

Civil Courts
Civil cases are heard in county courts and the High Court. Magistrates' courts have a concurrent jurisdiction with the county courts and the High Court in cases relating to children. There are some 250 county courts; cases are normally tried by judges sitting alone. The High Court deals with the more complicated civil cases. Its jurisdiction covers mainly civil cases and some criminal cases; it also deals with appeals from tribunals and from magistrates' courts in both civil and criminal matters. The three divisions of the High Court in the main sit at the Royal Courts of Justice in London.

Appeals from the High Court and county courts are heard in the Court of Appeal (Civil Division), and may go on to the House of Lords, the highest court of appeal.

The Home Secretary

The Home Secretary has overall responsibility for the criminal justice system in England and Wales and for advising the Queen on the exercise of the royal prerogative of mercy to pardon a person convicted of a crime or to remit all or part of a penalty imposed by a court.

Scotland

The principles and procedures of the Scottish legal system (particularly in civil law) differ in many respects from those of England and Wales. This stems, in part, from the adoption of elements of other European legal systems, based on Roman law, during the 16th century.

Criminal cases are tried in district courts, sheriff courts and the High Court of Justiciary. The main civil courts are the sheriff courts and the Court of Session.

The Secretary of State for Scotland recommends the appointment of all judges other than the most senior ones, appoints the staff of the High Court of Justiciary and the Court of Session, and is responsible for the composition, staffing and organisation of the sheriff courts. District courts are staffed and administered by the local authorities.

Northern Ireland

The legal system of Northern Ireland is in many respects similar to that of England and Wales.[18] It has its own court system: the superior courts are the Court of Appeal, the High Court and the Crown Court, which together comprise the Supreme Court of Judicature. The lower courts are the county courts and the

[18]For further details, see *Northern Ireland* (Aspects of Britain: HMSO, 1995).

magistrates' courts. A number of arrangements differ from those in England and Wales. A major example is that those accused of terrorist-type offences are tried in non-jury courts to avoid any intimidation of jurors.

Tribunals

Tribunals exercise judicial functions separate from the courts and are intended to be more accessible, less formal and less expensive. They are normally set up under statutory powers, which also govern their constitution, functions and procedure. Tribunals often consist of lay people, but they are generally chaired by a legally qualified person.

Some tribunals settle disputes between private citizens. Industrial tribunals, for example, have a major role in employment disputes. Others, such as those concerned with social security, resolve claims by private citizens against public authorities. A further group, including tax tribunals, decide disputed claims by public authorities against private citizens. Tribunals usually consist of an uneven number of people so that a majority decision can be reached.

In the case of some tribunals a two-tier system operates, with an initial right of appeal to a lower tribunal and a further right of appeal, usually on a point of law, to a higher one, and in some cases, to the Court of Appeal. Appeals from single-tier tribunals can usually be made only on a point of law to the High Court in England and Wales, to the Court of Session in Scotland, and to the Court of Appeal in Northern Ireland.

The independent Council on Tribunals exercises general supervision over many tribunals. A Scottish Committee of the Council exercises the same function in Scotland.

Britain and the European Union

Background to Britain's Membership

After the Second World War, the countries of Western Europe sought ways of working together to reconstruct their economies and to organise themselves in a way which would ensure that wars between them would not occur again. In 1952 Belgium, France, the Federal Republic of Germany, Italy, Luxembourg and The Netherlands established the supranational European Coal and Steel Community (ECSC). Although Britain decided not to participate, it established a practical working arrangement with the new body.

In 1957 the same six countries signed the Treaties of Rome, which established the European Economic Community (EEC) and the European Atomic Energy Community (EURATOM). Britain, along with six other countries, formed the European Free Trade Association (EFTA) in 1960. When it became clear that stronger links between EFTA and the European Community[19] were not being established, Britain began negotiations to join the Community in 1961. However, both these talks and a further application submitted in 1967 were blocked by French opposition.

Negotiations began again in 1970. The terms of entry were approved by Parliament in 1971. In 1972 Britain signed the Treaty of Accession, and on 1 January 1973 it became a member of the Community, at the same time as Denmark and the Irish

---

[19]The European Community comprised the ECSC, the EEC and EURATOM.

Republic. (Greece joined in 1981, Portugal and Spain in 1986, and Austria, Finland and Sweden in 1995.)

In 1974 the incoming Government renegotiated the terms of entry. It then recommended continued membership of the Community. This recommendation was endorsed by large majorities in both Houses of Parliament. In a referendum held in June 1975, 67.2 per cent of voters supported continued membership.

Following agreement on the need to make improvements in European co-operation, the Single European Act was passed in 1986. Its provisions included a target date of 1992 for completion of the internal market, an increased role for the European Parliament, and co-operation between member states on foreign policy.

Britain and its Community partners reached agreement on a Treaty on European Union at the European Council meeting in Maastricht in December 1991. The Treaty, which came into force on 1 November 1993, established the European Union, comprising the European Community and arrangements for inter-governmental co-operation on common foreign and security policies and on justice and home affairs.

Union Institutions

Council of the European Union
Major policy decisions are taken by the Council of the European Union. Member states are represented by the ministers appropriate to the subject under discussion.

The Presidency of the Council changes at six-monthly intervals; Britain assumed it for the fourth time from July to December 1992. In some cases decisions must be made unanimously; in others they are decided by a majority or a qualified majority, with votes weighted according to each country's size. Community policies are implemented by regulations, which are legally binding and directly applicable in all member countries; and directives, which are binding on member states but allow national authorities to decide on means of implementation.

Heads of Government of the member countries meet at least twice a year as the European Council. This takes important decisions and discusses EU policies and world affairs generally.

European Commission
The European Commission is composed of 20 commissioners (two from Britain) who are nominated by member governments and appointed by common agreement. It puts forward policy proposals, executes decisions taken by the Council of the European Union and ensures that European Union rules are correctly observed. The Commission is pledged to act independently of national or sectional interests.

European Parliament
The directly elected European Parliament has 626 members; Britain has 87 seats. The Parliament is consulted on a wide range of issues before the Council takes final decisions. The Commission can be removed from office as a whole by a two-thirds majority of all members of the Parliament. The Parliament adopts the Community's annual budget in agreement with the Council.

The European Parliament's powers were increased by the Single European Act and the Maastricht Treaty.

European Court of Justice

Each member state provides one of the judges to serve on the European Court of Justice, which is the final authority on all aspects of Community law. It interprets and adjudicates on the meaning of the treaties and on measures taken by the Council of the European Union and the Commission. It also hears complaints and appeals brought by or against Union institutions, member states or individuals and gives preliminary rulings on cases referred by courts in the member states.

The Court is assisted by a Court of First Instance, which handles certain cases brought by individuals and companies.

Court of Auditors

The Court of Auditors oversees the implementation of the Community's budget. It helps to counter waste and fraud. The Court consists of one member from each state.

Local Elections

Since 1996 British citizens have been able to vote and stand in the local elections of any country of the European Union, under the same conditions as nationals of that country, once those countries have passed the necessary domestic legislation.

Appendix 1: Government Departments and Agencies

An outline of the principal functions of the main government departments and executive agencies (see p. 62) is given below. Cabinet ministries are indicated by an asterisk. Executive agencies are normally listed under the relevant department, although in some cases they are included within the description of the departments' responsibilities.

The work of many of the departments and agencies listed below covers Britain as a whole. Where this is not the case, the following abbreviations are used:

—(GB) for functions covering England, Wales and Scotland;

—(E,W & NI) for those covering England, Wales and Northern Ireland;

—(E & W) for those covering England and Wales; and

—(E) for those concerned with England only.

The principal address and telephone number of each department are given. For details of the addresses of executive agencies see the *Civil Service Year Book*.

The Cabinet Office and the responsibilities of the Office of Public Service (OPS) are described on p. 48. The functions of the Welsh, Scottish and Northern Ireland Offices are outlined on pp. 83–97.

Cabinet Office (Office of Public Service)
70 Whitehall, London SW1A 2AS. Tel: 0171 270 1234

Executive Agencies
The Buying Agency
Central Computer and Telecommunications Agency
Chessington Computer Centre
Civil Service College
Occupational Health and Safety Agency
Property Advisers to the Civil Estate
Recruitment and Assessment Services
Security Facilities Executive

Two further agencies report to the Chancellor of the Duchy of Lancaster but are departments in their own right and not part of OPS. They are:
Central Office of Information (COI) (see p. 126)
Her Majesty's Stationery Office (HMSO) (see p. 126)

Economic Affairs

*Ministry of Agriculture, Fisheries and Food
3–8 Whitehall Place, London SW1A 2HH. Tel: 0171 270 3000
Policies for agriculture, horticulture, fisheries and food; responsibilities for related environmental and rural issues (E); food policies.

Executive Agencies
ADAS (Food, Farming, Land and Leisure)
Central Science Laboratory
Intervention Board
Meat Hygiene Service
Pesticides Safety Directorate
Veterinary Laboratories Agency
Veterinary Medicines Directorate

*Department of Trade and Industry
1–19 Victoria Street, London SW1H 0ET. Tel: 0171 215 5000
Industrial and commercial affairs; science and technology; promotion of new enterprise and competition; information about new business methods and opportunities; investor protection and consumer affairs. Specific responsibilities include innovation policy; regional industrial policy and inward investment promotion; small businesses; management best practice and business/education links; industrial relations and employment legislation; deregulation; international trade policy; commercial relations and export promotion; competition policy; company law; insolvency; radio regulation; patents and copyright protection (GB); the development of new sources of energy and the Government's relations with the energy industries.

Executive Agencies
Companies House
Insolvency Service
National Weights and Measures Laboratory
Patent Office
Radiocommunications Agency

*Department of Transport
Great Minster House, 76 Marsham Street, London SW1P 4DR. Tel: 0171 271 5000
Land, sea and air transport; domestic and international civil aviation; international transport agreements; shipping and the ports industry; marine pollution; regulation of drivers and vehicles (including road safety); regulation of the road haulage industry; transport and the environment. Motorways and trunk roads; oversight of local authority transport (E). Sponsorship of London Transport (E), British Rail; Railtrack (GB) and the Civil Aviation Authority.

Executive Agencies
Coastguard Agency
Driver and Vehicle Licensing Agency
Driving Standards Agency
Highways Agency
Marine Safety Agency
Transport Research Laboratory
Vehicle Certification Agency
Vehicle Inspectorate

*HM Treasury
Parliament Street, London SW1P 3AG. Tel: 0171 270 3000
Oversight of tax and monetary policy; planning and control of public spending; international financial relations; supervision of the financial system; and responsibility for a range of Civil Service management issues.

OTHER DEPARTMENTS
HM Customs and Excise
New King's Beam House, 22 Upper Ground, London SE1 9PJ. Tel: 0171 620 1313
Collecting and accounting for Customs and Excise revenues, including Value Added Tax; agency functions, including controlling certain imports and exports, policing prohibited goods, and compiling trade statistics.

ECGD (Export Credits Guarantee Department)
P.O. Box 2200, 2 Exchange Tower, Harbour Exchange Square, London E14 9GS. Tel: 0171 512 7000
Access to bank finance and provision of insurance for British project and capital goods exporters against the risk of not being paid for

goods and services; insurance cover for new British investment overseas; reinsurance to British-based private sector insurance companies offering insurance for consumer-type exports.

Inland Revenue
Somerset House, London WC2R 1LB. Tel: 0171 438 6622
Administration and collection of direct taxes; valuation of property (GB).

Executive Agency
Valuation Office

Office for National Statistics
Great George Street, London SW1P 3AQ. Tel: 0171 270 3000
The Office for National Statistics was created in April 1996 by the merger of the Central Statistical Office and the Office of Population, Censuses and Surveys. It is responsible for the full range of functions previously carried out by both former offices. This includes responsibility for:

—preparing and interpreting key economic statistics for government policy; collecting and publishing business statistics; publishing annual and monthly statistical digests;

—providing researchers, analysts and those in education and other customers with a statistical service which assists their work and promotes the functioning of industry and commerce;

—administration of the marriage laws and local registration of births, marriages and deaths (E & W); provision of population estimates and projections and statistics on health and other demographic matters (E & W); Census of Population (E & W). Surveys for other government departments and public bodies (GB); and

—promoting these functions within Britain, the European Union and internationally to provide a statistical service to meet European Union and international requirements.

Paymaster: The Office of HM Paymaster General
Sutherland House, Russell Way, Crawley, West Sussex RH10 1UH. Tel: 01293 560999
An executive agency providing banking services for government departments and the administration and payment of public service pensions.

Royal Mint
Llantrisant, Pontyclun, Mid Glamorgan CF72 8YT. Tel: 01443 222111
An executive agency responsible for producing and issuing coinage for Britain. It also produces, among other things, ordinary circulation coins and coinage blanks for around 100 countries as well as special proof and uncirculated quality collectors' coins, commemorative medals, and royal and official seals.

REGULATORY BODIES
Office of Electricity Regulation (OFFER)
Hagley House, Hagley Road, Birmingham B16 8QG. Tel: 0121 456 2100
Regulating and monitoring the electricity supply industry; promoting competition in the generation and supply of electricity; ensuring that companies comply with the licences under which they operate; protecting customers' interests (GB).

Office of Gas Supply (OFGAS)
Stockley House, 130 Wilton Road, London SW1V 1LQ. Tel: 0171
828 0898
Regulating and monitoring British Gas to ensure value for money
for customers, and granting licences to gas suppliers, shippers and
public gas transporters; enabling development of competition in the
industrial and domestic markets.

Office of the National Lottery (OFLOT)
2 Monck Street, London SW1P 2BQ. Tel: 0171 227 2000
Responsibility for the grant, variation and enforcement of licences
to run the National Lottery and promote lotteries as part of it.

Office for Standards in Education (OFSTED)
29–33 Kingsway, London WC2B 6SE. Tel: 0171 925 6800
Monitoring standards in English schools; regulating the work of
independent registered schools inspectors (E).

Office of Telecommunications (OFTEL)
50 Ludgate Hill, London EC4M 7JJ. Tel: 0171 634 8700
Monitoring telecommunications operators' licences; enforcing competition legislation; representing users' interests.

Office of Water Services (OFWAT)
Centre City Tower, 7 Hill Street, Birmingham B5 4UA. Tel: 0121
625 1300
Monitoring the activities of companies appointed as water and
sewerage undertakers (E & W); regulating prices, promoting economy
and efficiency, protecting customers' interests and facilitating competition. Ten regional customer service committees represent

customer interests and investigate their complaints. The OFWAT National Customer Council speaks for customers at a national level.

Legal Affairs

*The Lord Chancellor's Department
Selborne House, 54–60 Victoria Street, London SW1E 6QW. Tel: 0171 210 8500
Responsibility, through the Court Service, for the administration of the Supreme Court, county and crown courts and a number of tribunals. Also oversees the locally administered magistrates' courts and the Official Solicitor's Department. All work relating to judicial and quasi-judicial appointments. Overall responsibility for civil and criminal legal aid, for the Law Commission and for the promotion of general reforms in the civil law. Lead responsibility for private international law. The Lord Chancellor also has responsibility for the Northern Ireland Court Service; national archives (maintained by the Public Record Office—see below) and the Public Trust Office. Except for the Northern Ireland Court Service, the Lord Chancellor's remit covers England and Wales only. The Legal Services Ombudsman and the Advisory Committee on Legal Education and Conduct are independent of the Department but report to the Lord Chancellor.

Executive Agencies
The Court Service
HM Land Registry
Public Record Office
Public Trust Office

Crown Prosecution Service
50 Ludgate Hill, London EC4M 7EX. Tel: 0171 273 8000
An independent organisation responsible for the prosecution of criminal cases resulting from police investigations, headed by the Director of Public Prosecutions and accountable to Parliament through the Attorney General, superintending minister for the service (E & W).

Legal Secretariat to the Law Officers
Attorney General's Chambers, 9 Buckingham Gate, London SW1E 6JP. Tel: 0171 828 7155
Supporting the Law Officers of the Crown (Attorney General and Solicitor General) in their functions as the Government's principal legal advisers (E, W & NI).
The Attorney General, who is also Attorney General for Northern Ireland, is the Minister responsible for the Treasury Solicitor's Department (see p. 121), and has a statutory duty to superintend the Director of Public Prosecutions and the Director of the Serious Fraud Office (see p. 121), and the Director of Public Prosecutions for Northern Ireland.

Parliamentary Counsel
36 Whitehall, London SW1A 2AY. Tel: 0171 210 6633
Drafting of government Bills (except those relating exclusively to Scotland); advising departments on parliamentary procedure (E, W & NI).

HM Procurator General and Treasury Solicitor
Queen Anne's Chambers, 28 Broadway, London SW1H 9JS. Tel: 0171 210 3000

Provision of legal services to a large number of government departments, agencies, and public and quasi-public bodies. Services include litigation; giving general advice on interpreting and applying the law; instructing Parliamentary Counsel on Bills and drafting subordinate legislation and, through an executive agency, providing conveyancing services and property-related legal work (E & W).

Executive Agencies
Government Property Lawyers
Lord Advocate's Department and Crown Office (see p. 89)
The Treasury Solicitor's Department

Serious Fraud Office
Elm House, 10–16 Elm Street, London WC1X 0BJ. Tel: 0171 239 7272
Investigating and prosecuting serious and complex fraud under the superintendence of the Attorney General (E, W & NI).

External Affairs and Defence

*Ministry of Defence
Main Building, Horseguards Avenue, London SW1A 2HB. Tel: 0171 218 9000
Defence policy and control and administration of the armed services.

Defence Agencies
Army Base Repair Organisation
Army Base Storage and Distribution Agency
Army Individual Training Organisation

Army Technical Support Agency
Defence Analytical Services Agency
Defence Animal Centre
Defence Bills Agency
Defence Clothing and Textiles Agency
Defence Dental Agency
Defence Evaluation and Research Agency
Defence Postal and Courier Services Agency
Defence Transport and Movements Executive
Disposal Sales Agency
Duke of York's Royal Military School
Hydrographic Office
Joint Air Reconnaissance Intelligence
Logistic Information Systems Agency
Medical Supplies Agency
Meteorological Office
Military Survey
Ministry of Defence Police
Naval Aircraft Repair Organisation
Naval Recruiting and Training Agency
Pay and Personnel Agency
Queen Victoria School
RAF Maintenance Group
RAF Signals Engineering Establishment
RAF Training Group
Service Children's Education

*Foreign & Commonwealth Office
Downing Street, London SW1A 2AL. Tel: 0171 270 1500
Conduct of Britain's overseas relations, including advising on policy,

negotiating with overseas governments and conducting business in international organisations, promoting British exports and trade generally; administering aid (see below). Presenting British ideas, policies and objectives to the people of overseas countries; administering the remaining dependent territories; and protecting British interests and influence abroad, including the welfare of British citizens.

Executive Agency
Wilton Park Conference Centre

Overseas Development Administration
94 Victoria Street, London SW1E 5JL. Tel: 0171 917 7000
Responsibility for Britain's overseas aid to developing countries, for global environmental assistance, and also for the joint administration, with the Foreign & Commonwealth Office, of assistance to Central and Eastern Europe and the countries of the former Soviet Union. Responsibility for overseas superannuation.

Executive Agency
Natural Resources Institute

Social Affairs, the Environment and Culture

*Department for Education and Employment
Sanctuary Buildings, Great Smith Street, London SW1P 3BT. Tel: 0171 925 5000
Overall responsibility for school, college and university education (E). The Careers Service (E); Employment Service; youth and adult training policy and programmes; sponsorship of Training and

Enterprise Councils; European social policies and programmes; co-ordination of government policy on women's issues and equal opportunities issues in employment (GB).

Executive Agencies
Employment Service
Teachers' Pensions Agency

*Department of the Environment
2 Marsham Street, London SW1P 3EB. Tel: 0171 276 0900
Policies for local government finance and structure; local development; land-use planning; housing; construction industry; energy efficiency; environmental protection; water industry and the British Waterways Board; urban and rural regeneration; countryside and wildlife protection; legal and corporate services; Office of the Chief Scientist (E).

Executive Agencies
Building Research Establishment
Planning Inspectorate
Queen Elizabeth II Conference Centre

*Department of Health
Richmond House, 79 Whitehall, London SW1A 2NS. Tel: 0171 210 3000
National Health Service; personal social services provided by local authorities; and certain aspects of public health, including hygiene (E).

Executive Agencies
Medical Devices Agency
Medicines Control Agency
NHS Estates
NHS Pensions Agency

*Home Office
50 Queen Anne's Gate, London SW1H 9AT. Tel: 0171 273 3000
Administration of justice; criminal law; treatment of offenders, including probation and the prison service; the police; crime prevention; fire service and emergency planning; licensing laws; regulation of firearms and dangerous drugs; electoral matters and local legislation (E & W). Gaming (GB). Passports, immigration and nationality; race relations; royal matters. Responsibilities relating to the Channel Islands and the Isle of Man.

Executive Agencies
Fire Service College
Forensic Science Service
HM Prison Service
United Kingdom Passport Agency

*Department of National Heritage
2–4 Cockspur Street, London SW1Y 5DH. Tel: 0171 211 6000.
The arts; public libraries; national museums and galleries; tourism; sport; the built heritage (E); broadcasting; press regulation; film industry; export licensing of antiques; the National Lottery.

Executive Agencies
Historic Royal Palaces Agency
Royal Parks Agency

*Department of Social Security
Richmond House, 79 Whitehall, London SW1A 2NS. Tel: 0171 210 3000
The social security system (GB).

Executive Agencies
Benefits Agency
Child Support Agency
Contributions Agency
Information Technology Services Agency
War Pensions Agency

OTHER DEPARTMENTS AND AGENCIES
Central Office of Information (COI)
Hercules Road, London SE1 7DU. Tel: 0171 928 2345
An executive agency procuring publicity material and other information services on behalf of government departments and publicly funded organisations.

Her Majesty's Stationery Office (HMSO)
St Crispins, Duke Street, Norwich NR3 1PD. Tel: 01603 622211
An executive agency providing stationery, office machinery and furniture, printing and related services to Parliament, government departments and other public bodies. Publishing and selling government documents.

Ordnance Survey
Romsey Road, Southampton SO16 4GU. Tel: 01703 792000
An executive agency, which reports to the Secretary of State for the Environment, providing official surveying, mapping and associated scientific work covering Great Britain and some overseas countries.

Office of the Data Protection Registrar
Wycliffe House, Water Lane, Wilmslow, Cheshire SK9 5AF. Tel: 01625 545745
Maintains a public register of data users and computer bureaux; enforces the data protection principles; encourages the development of codes of practice to help data users comply with the principles; and considers complaints about breaches of the principles and other provisions of the Act. Data users must be registered with the Data Protection Registrar, an independent officer who reports directly to Parliament.

Appendix 2: The Privy Council

The Privy Council was formerly the chief source of executive power in the State; its origins can be traced back to the Curia Regis (or King's Court), which assisted the Norman monarchs in running the government. As the system of Cabinet government developed in the 18th century, however, much of the role of the Privy Council was assumed by the Cabinet, although the Council retained certain executive functions. Some government departments originated as committees of the Privy Council.

Nowadays the main function of the Privy Council is to advise the Queen on the approval of Orders in Council, including those made under prerogative powers, such as Orders approving the grant of royal charters of incorporation, and those made under statutory powers. Responsibility for each Order, however, rests with the Minister answerable for the policy concerned, regardless of whether he or she is present at the meeting where approval is given.

The Privy Council also advises the Sovereign on the issue of royal proclamations, such as those summoning or dissolving Parliament. The Council's own statutory responsibilities, which are independent of the powers of the Sovereign in Council, include supervising the registration authorities of the medical and allied professions.

Membership of the Council (retained for life, except for very occasional removals) is accorded by the Sovereign, on the recommendation of the Prime Minister (or occasionally, Prime Ministers of Commonwealth countries) to people eminent in public life—mainly politicians and judges—in Britain and the independent monarchies of the Commonwealth. Cabinet Ministers must be Privy Counsellors and, if not already members, are admitted to membership before taking their oath of office at a meeting of the Council. There are about 450 Privy Counsellors. A full Council is summoned only on the accession of a new Sovereign or when the Sovereign announces his or her intention to marry.

Committees of the Privy Council

There are a number of Privy Council committees. These include prerogative committees, such as those dealing with legislation from the Channel Islands (see p. 132) and the Isle of Man (see p. 135), and with applications for charters of incorporation. Committees may also be provided for by statute, such as those for the universities of Oxford and Cambridge and the Scottish universities. Membership of such committees is confined to members of the current administration. The only exceptions are the members of the Judicial Committee and the members of any committee for which specific provision authorises a wider membership.

Administrative work is carried out in the Privy Council Office under the Lord President of the Council, a Cabinet Minister.

The Judicial Committee of the Privy Council is primarily the final court of appeal for British dependent territories and those independent Commonwealth countries which have retained this avenue of appeal after independence. The Committee also hears appeals from the Channel Islands and the Isle of Man, and the disciplinary and health committees of the medical and allied professions. It has a limited jurisdiction to hear certain ecclesi-astical appeals. In 1995 the Judicial Committee heard 69 appeals and 69 petitions for special leave to appeal.

The members of the Judicial Committee include the Lord Chancellor, the Lords of Appeal in Ordinary, other Privy Coun-sellors who hold or have held high judicial office and certain judges from the Commonwealth.

Appendix 3: The Channel Islands and the Isle of Man

Relations with Britain

The distinction between the Channel Islands and the Isle of Man and other dependent territories has long been recognised by the British Government. In 1801, when government business connected with the colonies was transferred from the Secretary of State for the Home Department, business relating to the Channel Islands and the Isle of Man remained (and still rests) with the Home Secretary. Under the provisions of the British Nationality Act 1981 Channel Islanders and inhabitants of the Isle of Man enjoy full British citizenship.

The British Government is responsible for the foreign relations and external defence of the Channel Islands and the Isle of Man, and the Crown has ultimate responsibility for their good government. The Crown acts through the Privy Council, on the recommendation of Ministers operating in their capacity as Privy Counsellors. The island authorities are normally consulted when international agreements that might be binding on them as well as on Britain are under consideration by the British Government.

The Channel Islands and the Isle of Man are included by the Interpretation Act 1889 within 'the British Islands', and in the Merchant Shipping Acts trade with them is classed as 'Home Trade'. They use British currency together with locally issued currency in the same denominations.

Relations with the European Union

The position of the Channel Islands and the Isle of Man is governed by Articles 25–27 of the Act concerning the Conditions of Accession and by Protocol 3 to the Treaty of Accession. The Articles provide that the Community Treaties shall apply to the islands only to the extent described in the Protocol. The broad effect is that the islands are included in the European Union solely for customs purposes and for certain aspects of the Common Agricultural Policy.

The Channel Islands

The Channel Islands, situated off the north-west coast of France, are not part of Britain but dependent territories of the British Crown with their own legislatures (the States in Jersey, in Guernsey and in Alderney and the Chief Pleas in Sark), executives and judiciaries.

The Channel Islands consist of two Bailiwicks, Jersey and Guernsey. The latter includes the neighbouring islets of Herm and Jethou, together with Alderney and Sark. Each Bailiwick has a Lieutenant Governor, who is the personal representative of the Sovereign and the official channel of communication between Britain and the Island authorities. In both Jersey and Guernsey, the Bailiff, who is appointed by the Crown, presides over the Royal Court and the legislature and is the head of the island administration.

The total population of the islands is about 145,500.

History

The islands became part of the Duchy of Normandy in the 10th and 11th centuries, becoming dependent territories of the

English Crown when their Duke, William, became King of England in 1066. When continental Normandy was overrun by the King of France in 1204, the islands remained in the hands of the King of England, who continued to govern them in his capacity as Duke of Normandy until he surrendered the title in 1259. Thereafter the Sovereign continued to rule the islands as though he were Duke of Normandy, observing their laws, customs and liberties. These were later confirmed by the charters of successive sovereigns, which secured the islands their own judiciaries, freedom from the process of the English courts and certain other privileges. After the separation of the islands from Normandy, the local institutions were gradually moulded, largely on local initiative, to meet changing circumstances.

From 1204 onwards the islands were attacked and sometimes occupied by French forces on a number of occasions during hostilities between France and England. They were occupied by Germany during the Second World War.

System of Government and Law

The people of the Channel Islands are, with the exceptions mentioned in this chapter, responsible for their own affairs. Almost all island domestic legislation is made by their own legislatures. Island laws require approval by the Queen in Council (see p. 128) and are examined by the Home Office, in consultation with other government departments. The Home Secretary, as the Privy Counsellor with special responsibility for matters relating to the islands, then advises the Privy Council on whether Her Majesty in Council should make an assenting Order. Thus while in domestic affairs the islands form virtually independent democracies, their legislatures do not consist of their assemblies alone but each consists of the Queen, the Privy Council and the assembly.

Legislation passed by the British Parliament does not apply to the islands unless it contains express provision or necessary implication to that effect, or unless it has been extended to the islands by means of an Order in Council, generally made under an enabling provision in the Act. Consultations are held with the island authorities before the legislation is applied to their territories. Merchant shipping, aerial navigation, wireless telegraphy and nationality are examples of subjects on which British legislation applies to the islands.

The members of the States of Jersey and the States of Guernsey are elected directly by universal suffrage. There are two representatives from Alderney in the States of Guernsey.

Until the outbreak of the Second World War in 1939, Alderney was independent of Guernsey, although part of the Bailiwick. The island was evacuated in 1940. After the war, Guernsey took over responsibility for the airfield, education, health, immigration and the police services. The States of Alderney, which consists of an elected President and 12 elected members, still retains some legislative powers.

Although the States of Guernsey has power to legislate for Sark in some matters, Sark also has its own constitution, which is a unique mixture of feudal and popular government, with a hereditary 'Seigneur' at its head.

In addition to the States, Jersey and Guernsey have a system of local administration based on the parish (douzaine in Guernsey).

The basis of the laws of the Channel Islands is the common law of the Duchy of Normandy, as modified by local precedent and custom. In some respects, such as inheritance and bankruptcy, the law in the islands differs quite considerably from that in England. The Royal Courts in Jersey and Guernsey have full power to determine civil and criminal cases. In criminal cases appeal lies to the Courts of Appeal, which are constituted as separate courts for each Bailiwick, although they have a common panel of judges appointed by the Crown. The Judicial Committee of the Privy Council is the final court of appeal for civil and criminal cases. By arrangement with the British Government, some custodial sentences passed by the island courts are served in Britain.

The Home Secretary advises the Sovereign on the exercise of the prerogative of mercy in judicial matters arising in the islands.

The Isle of Man

The Isle of Man, which is situated in the Irish Sea off the coast of Cumbria, is not part of Britain but a dependent territory of the British Crown, with its own legislature (the Court of Tynwald), executive and judiciary. The Lieutenant Governor is appointed by and serves as the representative of the Crown. The population is about 70,000.

History
The island, an ancient kingdom, was under the general suzerainty of the kings of Norway until 1266, when it was ceded to Alexander III, King of Scotland. For the following 150 years it was the subject of claims by successive sovereigns of England and Scotland.

The English claim eventually prevailed, although there was no formal annexation by the English Crown. In 1405 Henry IV granted the island to Sir John Stanley and his heirs (who later became Earls of Derby). The Derby Lordship lasted, with one short interval, until 1736, when the Lordship passed, by inheritance, to the Murray family, the Dukes of Atholl. The Atholl interests in the island were bought out by the Crown, by statute, between 1765 and 1825.

The Isle of Man Purchase Act 1765, known as the 'Revestment Act', placed the island under the direct administration of the Crown. In 1866 the Isle of Man Customs, Harbours and Public Purposes Act separated the Manx revenues from those of Britain and gave Tynwald a limited control over island expenditure, subject to the approval of the Treasury and to the veto of the Lieutenant Governor. These provisions, which made available the finance necessary for public works in the island, were linked with the institution of a popularly elected legislative body, the House of Keys (see p. 137), hitherto self-nominated but thereafter elected for a term of years. The island now has control of its own revenues, and responsibility for the provision of most services rests with Departments of Tynwald (see below).

System of Government and Law

The people of the Isle of Man are, in general, responsible for their own affairs, with the exceptions already mentioned, and almost all domestic legislation is made by Tynwald. The Lieutenant Governor has delegated power to grant Royal Assent to legislation dealing with domestic matters, and there is provision for those laws which transcend the frontiers of the island to be reserved for Royal Assent by the Queen in Council (see p. 128).

Island laws are examined by the Home Office in consultation with other government departments in order to determine whether Royal Assent may properly be given. In the case of legislation which is to be reserved, the Home Secretary then advises the Privy Council whether Her Majesty in Council should make an assenting Order. Thus, while in domestic affairs the island forms a virtually independent democracy, its legislature does not consist of Tynwald alone but of the Queen, the Privy Council and Tynwald.

Legislation passed by the British Parliament does not apply to the island unless it contains express provision or necessary implication to that effect, or unless it has been extended to the island by means of an Order in Council, generally made under an enabling provision in the Act. Consultations are held with the Government of the Isle of Man before the legislation is applied to the island. Merchant shipping, aerial navigation, wireless telegraphy and nationality are examples of the subjects on which British legislation applies to the Isle of Man.

The Court of Tynwald, claimed to be 1,000 years old in 1979 and to be the oldest legislature in the world, consists of the Lieutenant Governor; the Legislative Council, which includes members indirectly elected by the House of Keys and certain *ex-officio* members; and the House of Keys, an assembly of 24 members elected by universal adult suffrage. A Council of Ministers (formerly the Executive Council) appointed under the Council of Ministers Act 1990 from members of Tynwald acts in all matters of government. The Lieutenant Governor's earlier functions (for example, presiding over Tynwald and in government through the Governor in Council role) have now been removed.

The Manx judicial system has three tiers—the magistrates' courts, the Manx High Court and the Manx Court of Appeal. The Judge of Appeal is appointed by the Crown. The Judicial Committee of the Privy Council is the final court of appeal for civil and criminal cases. The two Manx judges, who are also appointed by the Crown, are known as Deemsters (derived from their function of giving a 'doom' or judgment). By arrangement with the British Government, some custodial sentences passed by the island's courts are served in Britain. The Home Secretary advises the Sovereign on the exercise of the prerogative of mercy in judicial matters arising in the island.

Further Reading

General

Aspects of Britain series

Britain's Legal Systems (2nd edn)	HMSO	1996
Government and the Individual: *The Citizen's Means of Redress*	HMSO	1996
Human Rights (2nd edn)	HMSO	1996
Organisation of Political Parties (2nd edn)	HMSO	1994
Pressure Groups	HMSO	1994

Other

The Administrative Process in Britain. Brown, R. G. S. and Steel, D. R. (2nd edn)	Methuen: Routledge	1979
British System of Government. Birch, Anthony H. (9th edn)	Routledge	1990
Constitutional and Administrative Law. Smith, S. A. De, Street, H. and Brazier, R. (7th edn)	Penguin	1994
First Report of the Committee on Standards in Public Life (Nolan Report). Cm 2850	HMSO	1995

Governing Britain: A Guidebook to Political Institutions. Hanson, A. H. and Walles, M.	Fontana Press	1990
The Government's Response to the First Report from the Committee on Standards in Public Life. (Cm 2931)	HMSO	1995
Public Administration in Britain Today. Greenwood, J. R. and Wilson, D. J.	Unwin Hyman	1989

Monarchy

The Crown Estate: The Commissioners' Report (annual) *Report of the Royal Trustees.*	HMSO	1993
The Monarchy (2nd edn: Aspects of Britain series).	HMSO	1996
The Oxford Illustrated History of the British Monarchy, Cannon, John and Griffiths, Ralph.	Oxford University Press	1988
The Royal Encyclopaedia: The Authorised Book of the Royal Family, Allison, Ronald and Riddell, Sarah (eds).	Macmillan	1991
Royal Heritage–The Reign of Queen Elizabeth II. Plumb, J. H. and Wheldon, Huw.	Chancellor	1985

Parliament

Factsheets on various aspects of the House of Commons and its work, including a list of MPs and Ministers, are available free from the Public Information Office, House of Commons, London SW1A 0AA.

Factsheets on various aspects of the House of Lords and its work are available free from the Journal and Information Office, House of Lords, London SW1A 0PW.

The Commons under Scrutiny, Ryle, Michael and Richards, Peter (eds).	Routledge	1988
Dod's Parliamentary Companion, (annual).	Dod's Parliamentary Companion Ltd	
The House of Lords, Shell, Donald.	Harvester Wheatsheaf	1992
How Parliament Works, Silk, Paul (with Walters, Rhodri).	Longman	1989
Member of Parliament: the Job of a Backbencher, Radice, L., Vallance, E. and Willis, V.	Macmillan	1987
Parliament (3rd edn: Aspects of Britain series).	HMSO	1996
Parliament, Griffiths, J. A. G. and Ryle, Martin.	Sweet & Maxwell	1989
Parliament Today, Adonis, Andrew.	Manchester University Press	1990
Parliamentary Elections (2nd edn). (Aspects of Britain series).	HMSO	1995

Parliamentary Commissioner for Administration: Annual Report.	HMSO	
Parliamentary Practice (A Treatise on the Law, Privileges, Proceedings and Usage of Parliament), May, Sir Thomas Erskine. (21st edn), edited by Clifford T. J. Boulton.	Butterworth	1989
The Times Guide to the House of Commons, Wood, Alan and Wood, Roger, 1992.	Times Books	1992

Prime Minister, Cabinet, Government Departments and the Civil Service

British Government and Politics, (6th edn). Punnett, R. M.	Dartmouth	1994
Cabinet, Hennessy, Peter	Basil Blackwell	1986
Citizen's Charter: The Facts and Figures. (Cm 2970)	HMSO	1995
The Citizen's Charter: Raising the Standard, (Cm. 1599).	HMSO	1991
The Civil Service (Aspects of Britain series).	HMSO	1994
Civil Service Commissioners' (Annual Report).	HMSO	
The Civil Service: Continuity and Change. (Cm 2627)	HMSO	1994
Civil Service Statistics. (Annual).	HMSO	

The Civil Service: Taking Forward Continuity and Change (Cm 2748)	HMSO	1995
The Civil Service Today, Drewry, Gavin and Butcher, Tony.	Blackwell	1991
Civil Service Year Book (Annual).	HMSO	
Competitiveness: Forging Ahead (Cm 2867)	HMSO	1995
The Government and Politics of Britain. Mackintosh, John P. Edited by P. G. Richards. (7th edn).	Unwin Hyman: Routledge	1988
History and Functions of Government Departments (Aspects of Britain series).	HMSO	1993
Improving Management in Government: The Next Steps, (A report to the Prime Minister).	HMSO	1988
Next Steps: Agencies in Government Review (Annual). HMSO		
Open Government. (Cm 2290).	HMSO	1993
Public Bodies (Annual)	HMSO	
Quangos in Britain. Governments and the Networks of Public Policy Making. Barker, Anthony (ed).	Macmillan	1982
Reforming the Civil Service, Fry, Geoffrey, K.	Edinburgh University Press	1993
Setting Up Next Steps. (A short account of the origins, launch and implementation of the Next Steps Project in the British Civil Service.)	HMSO	1991

Spending Public Money:
Governance and Audit Issues (Cm 3179) HMSO   1996

Whitehall   Secker &
                                       Warburg   1989

The Whitehall Companion (Annual).   Dods

Local Government

The Conduct of Local Authority
Business: The Government Response to
the Report of the Widdicombe Committee
of Inquiry.   HMSO   1988

A History of Local Government in the
Twentieth Century Keith-Lucas,
Bryan, and Richards, Peter G.   Allen & Unwin 1978

Local Government (Aspects of Britain
series)   HMSO   1996

Local Government in Britain:
Everyone's Guide to How It All Works,
Byrne, Anthony. (5th edn).   Penguin   1990

Local Government in Wales:
A Charter for the Future. (Cm 2155). HMSO   1993

The Local Government System,
Richards, Peter G.   Allen & Unwin 1983

Report of the Committee of Inquiry into
the Conduct of Local Authority Business,
(Chairman: Mr David Widdicombe,
QC.)   HMSO   1986

Research Vol 1: The Political Organisation of Local Authorities.	HMSO	1986
Research Vol II: The Local Government Councillor.	HMSO	1986
Research Vol III: The Local Government Elector.	HMSO	1986
Research Vol IV: Aspects of Local Democracy.	HMSO	1986
Reviewing Local Government in the English Shires: A Progress Report.	HMSO	1993
Scotland in the Union: A Partnership for Good. (Cm 2225).	HMSO	1993

Index

Printed in the United Kingdom for The Stationery Office
Dd. 302426 C30 11/96 9385 4683